Contents

First published in Italy
Edizioni del Canal (Canal Books)
Via Jacopo Cavalli 1, Lido Venice, Italy
Printed by Stamperia di Venezia, Venice, Italy

FIRST U.S. EDITION

STANDARD BOOK NUMBER: 06-430021-8

LIBRARY OF CONGRESS CATALOG CARD NUMBER: 75-180865

101 Buildings to See in Venice

Antonio Salvadori

Translated from the Italian
by Brenda Balich

ICON EDITIONS

Harper & Row, Publishers
New York, Evanston, San Francisco, London

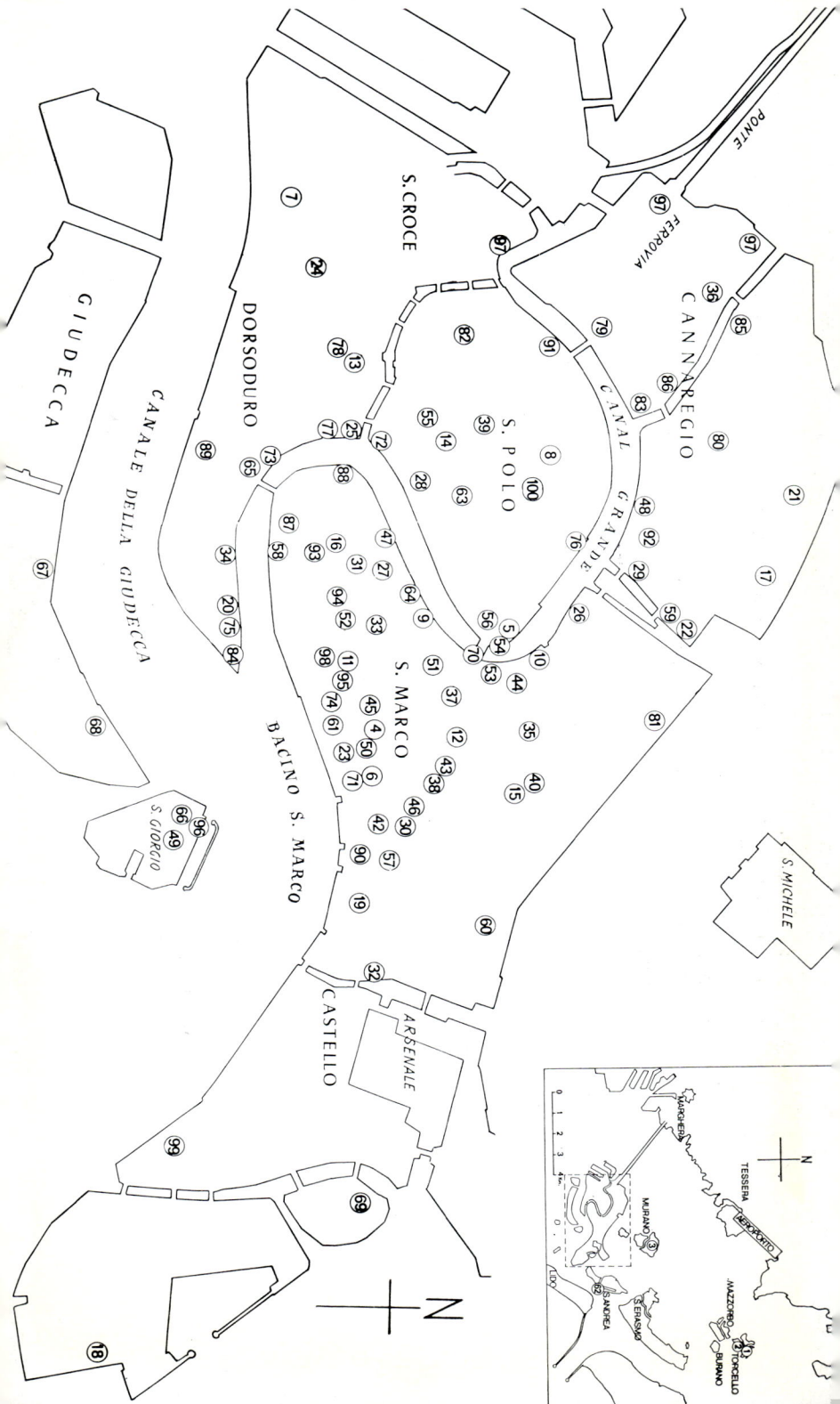

GIUDECCA

S. CROCE

DORSODURO

CANALE DELLA GIUDECCA

CANNAREGIO

FERROVIA

PONTE

CANAL GRANDE

S. POLO

S. MARCO

BACINO S. MARCO

S. GIORGIO

CASTELLO

ARSENALE

S. MICHELE

N

MARGHERA

TESSERA

MURANO

S. ANDREA

S. ERASMO

MAZZORBO BURANO

TORCELLO

LIDO

0 1 2 3 4 5

Foreword

This book is intended as an instrument to guide the visitor interested in architecture. The choice of the examples illustrated here is obviously limited by the theme of this series, 101 buildings; it includes however all the most celebrated monuments, and an effort has been made to give an outline as complete as possible of the development of Venetian architecture as a whole, emphasising the most significant buildings and periods. This volume is however a selection and it reflects, as do all selections, the personal taste of the author.

We hope that this small book may be found useful also to those readers who already know the city and who will appreciate the considerable number of illustrations rarely to be found collected in a book of this size and price.

Though the theme of the volume is precisely defined, and in a way exclusive, the historical and aesthetic significance of urban planning has not been forgotten. A city is not only a collection of buildings; it has its own environment which is often more precious than the individual buildings which create it. The urban development of Venice has been more specifically outlined in the introduction.

INTRODUCTION

The characteristics peculiar to Venetian architecture are the result of various factors; some due to local traditions, others to its particular environment, and still others deriving from different civilisations with which the Venetians came in contact.

The local tradition was formed in the lagoon based on Roman style of buildings. Fleeing from barbaric invasions, the communities who made up the first nucleus of Venice came from the Roman towns of Padua, Oderzo, Aquileia and, especially, Altino. The appearance of the Venetian house, for example, reflects that of the Roman country house (Bettini), many of which were to be found at Altino. The Ravenna tradition, too, can be considered a local one, in so far as the Duchy of Venice depended, at least during the early period, on Ravenna. Religious architecture (Torcello) and the style of mosaic decoration, which developed in Venice, was derived in fact from Ravenna.

The Benedictine building tradition, with its economic and social organisation, had also been established in the lagoon since the ninth century; it was one of the most important components of the urban composition of Venice, when the communities were transferred to the Rialto islands from the more vulnerable settlements dispersed at Malamocco, Eraclea, Jesolo, Torcello, etc.

a) **Ravenna.** Church of S. Apollinare.
b) **Tessera** (Venice). Church with XIth century bell-tower.
c) **Altino.** Roman road.

The archipelago of the Rialto islands, in the centre of the lagoon, was the first nucleus of the present-day city of Venice. They were small islands round some distributaries of the Brenta (the present-day Grand Canal and Giudecca Canal); tiny strips of land, hardly higher than the level of the water, divided by innumerable small winding canals, continually swept by the ebb and flow of the tides. Other strips of land had been formed over the centuries enlarging the city, always, however, following the courses of the original canals, to enable them to use the layer of clay and sand («caranto») as a foundation for new buildings. The townscape peculiar to Venice and its architecture are both derived from these hydrographic conditions.

Besides factors of tradition and environment, styles coming from other civilisations, Byzantium and the Middle East, have helped to form Venetian architecture. The crusades, trade with countries on the shores of the Mediterranean, merchants' long journeys in the lands of central Asia, and even China (Marco Polo), all enlarged and enriched traditional horizons and tastes. It is understandable how the echoes of Romanesque and Gothic art and architecture from the continent, reached sea-girt Venice late and only indirectly, brought during the XIVth century, especially by religious orders.

a

b

c

a) **Corte del Remer.** Pointed arches (XIIIth century) which show both Byzantine and Arabic influences.

b) **Campo del Milion.** Horse-shoe arch (XI-XIIth century) derived from Arabic architecture.

c) **Fondaco dei Turchi.** The scheme of the façade (heavily restored, in fact practically rebuilt in the last century) recalls the Roman villas at Altino. Loggia and arches of this building, originally erected in the Byzantine style, are in the Byzantine style, XIIth century,

This « time lag » in the stylistic evolution of Venetian architecture, which was to last until the XVth century, can also been explained by the strongly conservative character of the Venetians themselves. Merchants and seamen, used to living in a place like the lagoon with few natural resources, Venetians have never had a tendency to be extravagant, and certainly not with building materials, which were brought to Venice from a distance with great difficulty: the wood from the mountain forests, bricks from the mainland and stone from the Istrian coast.

Venice is an « artificial » city, « a city born adult », as Elena Bassi says with reason; not only building methods, but also building materials and architectural fragments were brought from the abandoned centres of Altino, Torcello, Jesolo, etc. The habit, even the necessity of re-using old materials salvaged from ancient buildings persisted. The example of small Roman bricks, « altinelle », brought from Altino to Torcello, then from Torcello to Venice, and there taken from Veneto-byzantine buildings to make Gothic constructions, and again used in later centuries, is typical. The example of secular buildings, with Veneto-Byzantine walls, modified with an additional storey added in Gothic style, with the main façade rebuilt applying Renaissance or Baroque marble facing, is also typical. The constructional technique and the interior distribution of Venetian buildings have therefore remained unchanged, those which experience had shown to be best adapted to the special requirements of the city and its environment. The same can be said of the town planning of Venice; even if the city grew larger its original appearance underwent few substantial modifications.

a) **SS. Giovanni e Paolo.** The Greek marble columns of the portal came from Torcello.

b) **Corte del Remer.** Wall of a Veneto-Byzantine house built with "altinelle", roman bricks (5x10x20 cm. in size) from Altino.

c) **Church of S. Vidal.** Stone with Roman inscription at the base of the bell tower.

10

The main development in the evolution of Venetian architecture took place in the XVth and XVIth centuries, a direct consequence of the new political and economic situation. Its overseas trade and possessions, which had made Venice's fortune, were being abandoned one by one under the threat of Turkish power; 'pari passu' the interests and enterprises of the Venetian Republic were being transferred to the continent. This period saw Venice's military, political and, above all, economic expansion on the mainland: capital prudently recalled to the homeland was reinvested in the cities and provinces of the Veneto. We thus see various concomitant phenomena: the first is the development and transformation of building in the city, with an ever-increasing rhythm and with even more imposing and magnificent buildings.

The second phenomenon is the arrival in Venice, from other cities and regions, and even from beyond the Alps, of artists and craftsmen, including architects and stone masons, with the consequent train of new ideas and up-to-date techniques which would have been unthinkable until then. This stream of artists and architects emanated, as well as from the Veneto, from Tuscany and above all from Lombardy, mainly from the Lugano, Como and Bergamo areas, in whole family groups (e.g. the Reverti, Lombardo, Fantoni, Bregno, Coducci, Rizzo, Buora, Bon, Dei Grigi, Scarpagnino, Contino, etc.).

A third phenomenon is the transfer of the organisational and building capacity of the Venetians to large agricultural estates, which

brought about the architecture of the innumerable country houses in the Veneto area. Just as the Venetian house was the headquarters of commercial firms as well as residence, thus the Venetian country house, besides being a holiday retreat, was also the headquarters of the farm. The central block repeats the tripartite plan of the city house, but at either side stand lower wings, often with porticoes (« barchesse »), where store rooms, etc., of the farm were situated. As in the Venetian house, the servants, employees and farm workers all lived together in a patriarchal system of communal living.

a

b

c

a) **Vicenza.** Villa Rotonda by Palladio (1551).

b) **Fanzolo** (Treviso). Villa Emo by Palladio (1560).

c) **Barcon** (Treviso). "Barchessa" of Villa Pola, an XVIIth century country house perhaps by Massari, still used as a farm building.

Among the various kinds of buildings in Venice at this time, there are the usual ones of a civic or private nature, like the « casafontego », or public buildings like the offices of the various magistratures, such as the Procuratie, the Prisons, the Camerlenghi Palace, the Fabbriche di Rialto, etc., and the churches and convents. Besides these particular buildings, others were erected, half secular, half religious, half public, half private: these are the « scuole » or guild halls. These guilds were associations with a religious, corporate function of mutual assistance, or assemblies for the numerous foreign communities working in Venice. They were divided into devotional and arts and crafts schools; we thus have, among the religious ones, the Scuola di S. Marco, di S. Giovanni Evangelista and di S. Rocco; and the « Scuole » of the Laneri, the Battiloro, or the Bombardieri, amongst the arts and crafts guilds. The confraternities which gathered round the guilds were numerous (in the XVIIIth century there were 425 of them, divided into 150 arts and crafts and 275 religious ones). They were frequently of great social importance, and sometimes very wealthy indeed, hence their halls were important buildings from an architectural point of view, sometimes even magnificent like the six « Scuole Grandi » (Scuola della Carità, di S. Giovanni Evangelista, di S. Marco, di S. Rocco, della Misericordia, di S. Teodoro, to which that of the Carmini was later added), their interiors all decorated by precious works of art. Large or small, the guild buildings had a common plan: they were on two floors, with a hall and side rooms on each floor, joined by a great stairway. They remain today the spontaneous expression of the communal capacity for self-government of the Venetian people and of their extraordinary love for all art forms.

In the panorama of Venetian architecture some typically functional buildings should be mentioned, like the « fonteghi », e.g. dei Tedeschi and dei Turchi; and the warehouses, like that « del megio » (millet) on the Grand Canal, or of the salt on the Zattere, others for grain on Giudecca and on the Riva degli Schiavoni, real silos for strategic reserves of food. The most important group of functional buildings is however the Arsenal, which from an architectural point of view is extraordinarily interesting. Enlarged and rebuilt several times during the course of the centuries, it was the heart of naval powers of the Republic.

The Arsenal was jealously guarded and isolated by its surrounding walls and towers, and contains several stretches of water of varying sizes, the docks, and forms an autonomous urban unit, almost a town within a town. The difference between the castles of medieval towns and the Arsenal of Venice is that the latter was not purely defensive, but a large shipbuilding yard: an industrial plant for the construction of ships, which, in their turn, were the source of power and wealth for the Republic.

All buildings in Venice, of whatever kind, are served by a double transport network, by water and by land. The meeting point of these two kinds of transport is the bridge. The bridges of Venice, too, have their history,

Scuola dei Battiloro (Goldsmiths Guild). An XVIIIth century building on the Grand Canal.

Magazzini del Megio (Millet warehouse) on the Grand Canal, built in the XVth century.

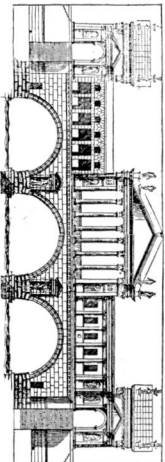

a) Palladio's project for the Rialto Bridge.

the evolution of the various types and their architectural value. From the ramp bridges for horses to the bridge with steps, from bridges without parapets, like that of Torcello, which were common right up to the XVIIIth century, to bridges with balustrades, low walls or railings. From the primitive arched brick constructions, they progressed to those in Istrian stone, with up to three arches, like the one designed by Tirali at S. Giobbe.

In some the stone is limited to the bearing arch, others are entirely in stone, like the Ponte della Paglia. Bridges can become an imposing part of the townscape like that of Rialto. In the XIXth century iron bridges began to be built in Venice, and this material, with its light visible structure, was eminently suitable to the city, like the one in front of San Pietro di Castello, one of the finest of its kind.

b) Ponte dei tre Archi by Tirali on the Cannaregio Canal (1688).

c) Bridge without parapet on Rio S. Felice.

d) Bridge at S. Giacomo dall'Orio.

e) The XIXth century iron bridge at S. Pietro di Castello.

13

The townscape of Venice offers very many kinds of spatial and figurative schemes, of different complexity. There is the « rio », the frequently curving canal lined by buildings, then that flanked by one or two «fondamente» (waterside streets), the bank of the canal on which stand houses, in a single transport system. Then there is the « calle », narrow foot path for pedestrians only, and the wider streets, « calle larga », « salizzada », « ruga », between lines of shops, the last two named usually busy shopping centres. The markets in the various quarters are usually to be found in the squares of Venice, « campi », round which normally stand the church and other important buildings. These squares are autonomous urban centres, always served by canals, but are of different dimensions. The largest, like S. Polo or S. Maria Formosa, were also used for popular fairs like bullfights. Small squares of a residential nature, « campielli », are the centres of everyday social intercourse. Round these urban spaces are grouped popular houses and wealthy residences, and even « palazzetti », one next to the other. In a study of the townscape of Venice, the architecture of the more modest buildings, the so called « Venezia minore » (intelligently studied by Egle Trincanato), cannot therefore be separated from the more important elaborate architecture, without neglecting the real fascination of the city.

The history of Venetian architecture, up to the end of the Republic, is made up of many small transformations, additions, or rebuildings; care was taken not to waste what was good and useful, out of business caution

rather than out of respect for the culture and taste of the past. « Che el sia fato che el staga ben », to be made so that it looks good, was the approval for the new buildings. In this way Venetian architecture passed without shocks and without deviating from its true nature through the winds of change of the Renaissance, the Baroque and Neo-Classicism. It displays an extraordinary capacity for assimilation and transformation, almost corrosion, of widely different styles and tastes, by means of light, 'chiaroscuro' and colour; this is perhaps the real unifying continuity of the Venetian tradition.

The architecture of Venice has reached us today practically intact, despite some unfortunate XIXth century rebuilding. Attempts have been made to introduce modern architecture into this ancient fabric, but the results, apart from a few isolated examples, have not been encouraging up to now. It is a positive sign, however, that some of the most celebrated contemporary architects have participated enthusiastically in three interesting projects for new buildings in Venice: Frank Lloyd Wright made a design for the Palazzina Masieri on the Grand Canal (which unfortunately was never built), and, more recently, Le Corbusier designed the new Hospital at San Giobbe, on which work should soon start. Finally Louis Kahn has produced a fascinating project for a Conference Centre and a new pavilion for the Biennale in the Giardini. These projects, while differing in importance and character, do show the vitality of Venice, whose architectural and town planning problems always rouse great international in-

a) Market in Campo S. Maria Formosa.

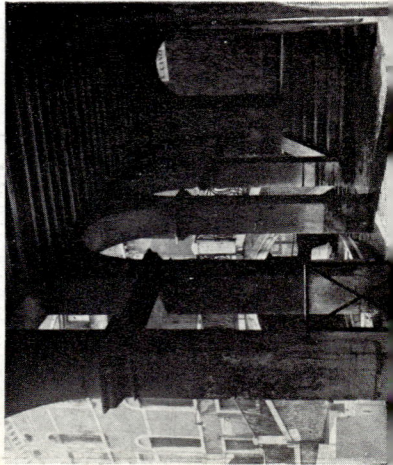

b) "Sottoportego" along the Rio dei SS. Apostoli.

terest. These projects also indicate how the solution of the problems of Venice, never an easy matter, is to be sought in the field of ideas and personalities far wider than the strictly Venetian or Italian horizon, as, moreover, has often happened in the long history of Venetian architecture.

Le Corbusier: project for the new hospital at S. Giobbe.

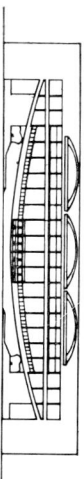

Louis Kahn: project for Convention Hall (a) and Italian Pavilion (b) in the Biennale gardens.

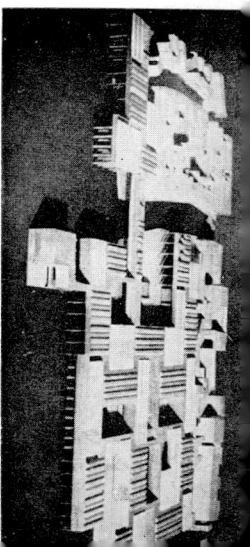

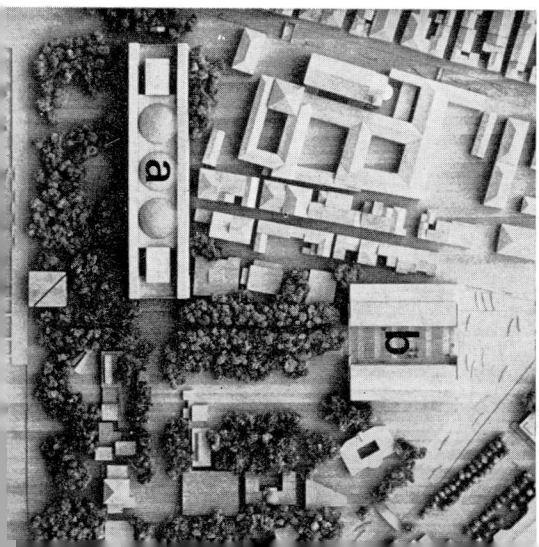

BIBLIOGRAPHICAL NOTE

Guide Books

G. Lorenzetti - Venice and its Lagoon (Istituto Poligrafico dello Stato, 1956).

H. Honour - The Companion Guide to Venice (Collins, 1965).

G. Piamonte - Venezia vista dall'acqua (Stamperia di Venezia Editrice, 1966).

On architecture

P. Paoletti - Architettura e scultura del Rinascimento a Venezia (Ongania, 1893).

E. Trincanato - Venezia Minore (Edizioni del Milione, 1948).

J. Ruskin - The Stones of Venice (1851).

E. Bassi - Architettura del Sei e Settecento a Venezia (E.S.I., 1962).

R. Wittkower - Art and Architecture in Italy 1600-1750 (Pelican History of Art, 1958).

R. Wittkower - Architectural Principles in the Age of Humanism (Tiranti, 1962).

F. Haskell - Patrons and Painters (Chatto & Windus, 1963).

R. Pane - Palladio (1948).

S. Muratori - Studi per una operante storia Urbana di Venezia (I.P.S., 1959).

P. Maretto - Edilizia Gotica Veneziana (I.P.S., 1960).

Brunetti, Bettini, Fiocco, Forlati - Torcello (Alfieri).

S. Bettini - S. Marco (Tre Venezie Editrice, 1946).

History

R. Cessi - Storia di Venezia (Centro Arti e Costume, Venezia).

L. Luzzato - Storia Economica di Venezia (Centro Arti e Costume, Venezia).

M. Berengo - La Società Veneta alla fine del Settecento (Firenze, 1955).

J. Morris - Venice (Faber and Faber, 1960).

101 BUILDINGS

TORCELLO

The history of Torcello precedes that of Venice; in fact this political and commercial centre, founded in the early Middle Ages as an offshoot of the Roman Altino, having its greatest development between the seventh and the fourteenth centuries, was one of the parent cities of the Venetian Republic. Its decadence was caused by the silting-up of this part of the lagoon, by the unhealthy climate which developed there, and by the exodus of its population to Murano and Venice.

Almost all the buildings which existed on the main island and on the surrounding ones (e.g. Costanziaca, Ammiana, etc.) were gradually destroyed, and the building materials, together with the various pieces of decoration were carried off to Venice, and used again in various ways in the new city.

Some of the buildings still remaining in Tor-

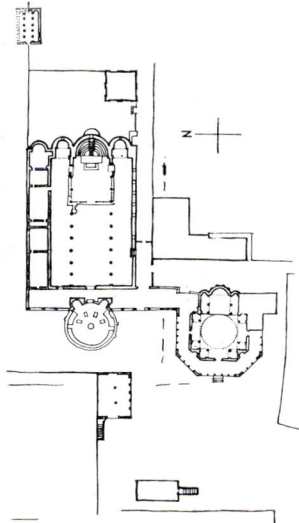

cello, therefore, represent in a sense, the pre-history of the architecture of Venice. The remains of the Baptistery are reminiscent of the late Roman tradition; the Basilica of Santa Maria Assunta, proto-christian in character with exarchal developments, bears witness to the pre-byzantine periods. The church of Santa Fosca combines the teachings of late byzantine architecture with the Venetian Romanesque style; the campanile is an example of this, and perhaps an echo is to be found in the basilichetta of San Marco.

The arrangement of these various religious buildings follows the usual early Christian plan: the cathedral has the baptistery immediately in front of it, and at the side, instead of at the rear, the "Martyrion", in this case Santa Fosca.

The secular buildings stood in front of the religious ones to form the "piazza"; they are represented today by the Palazzetto del Consiglio, and the Palazzo dell'Archivio, both of a later date than the religious buildings.

1

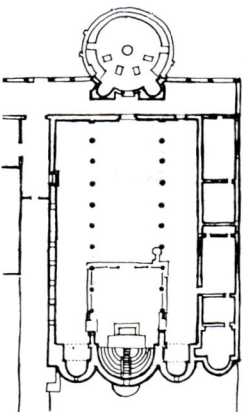

CATHEDRAL OF SANTA MARIA ASSUNTA, VII c. The 'Cathedra' of Torcello is considered to be the oldest monument in the islands of the lagoon, having been founded in 639 by Bishop Mauro who transferred the Diocese of Altino there. The original church, early Christian in character, built on the model of the churches of Ravenna, did not differ greatly from the present one, a central semi-circular apse, side apses ('diaconico' and 'protesi') which were probably rectangular, and a raised presbytery. In front of the façade, standing in line with the church, are the remains of the Baptistery, which, too, dates from the seventh century, built on a circular plan like the Roman thermal baths. The church was restored, the first time, by Bishop Adeodato, with the addition of the central part of the portico (the side parts date from the fourteenth century). The central apse was rebuilt, the circular crypt below it, and the side apses with shallow external pilasters. The church was restored again in 1008 by Bishop Orseolo (son of the famous Doge), with the raising of the whole building, as can be detected from the exterior of the façade, from the thickening of the interior walls, and from the transformation of the arches in the nave. The present mosaic floor dates from this period: an earlier floor, 20 centimetres below, has been found underneath. The Choir, the side ambos, and the Iconostasis (but the paintings date from the fifteenth century) were all rebuilt, sometimes using earlier fragments. In the recent restoration (1929) the altar table of the seventh century was restored to its place over a Roman arch containing the remains of St. Eliodoro; thus the steps of the eleventh century apse are more easily seen, with the Bishop's cattedra in the centre.

Despite repeated restorations and additions, the interior of Santa Maria Assunta retains the simple, solemn beauty of the exarch churches. The mosaics are inseparable from the architecture, that of the 'diaconico' inspired by a similar one in San Vitale in Ravenna, dates from the seventh century; the other mosaics in the same apse date from the ninth century. The twelve apostles above the apse steps belong to the twelfth century, they echo the rhythm of the arches of the nave; the Madonna Teotoca in the cove of the central apse is of the thirteenth century, forming an ideal pivot of all the interior space. The huge mosaic of the "Last Judgment" dates from the thirteenth century; it serves to counter-balance the mosaics of the apse.

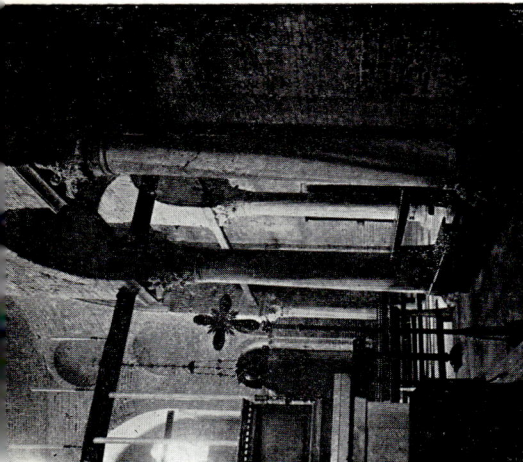

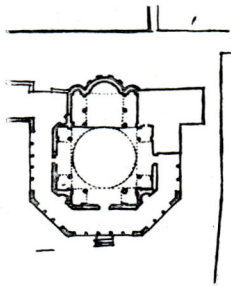

2

SANTA FOSCA, XI c. This church was built at the end of the eleventh century and the beginning of the twelfth, it is practically co-eval with St. Mark's and San Donato of Murano. It was originally intended to be a "martyrion": a small church built on a central plan, containing the bodies of martyrs, and together with the baptistery and the basilica made up the symbolic trilogy of early Christian buildings (birth, life, and death). Santa Fosca is in the form of a Greek cross, with its eastern arm elongated, opening onto three apses. The four barrel vaults rest on the corner arching, and on the two small aisles one at either side of the altar. There was once a large brick cupola, supported by the vaults and by double squinches; the cupola has now been replaced by a wooden roof. The interior, based on Byzantine principles of construction, can be seen to be extraordinarily coherent, structurally and spatially. The exterior octagonal portico, whose function was to balance the thrust of the cupola and the vaults, further enlarges the interior space. At the back, the three small apses, simpler in form than those of S. Donato and St. Mark's, give an air of refinement and harmony which is oriental in flavour. Even with its modest dimensions, and in its utter simplicity, this church can be considered one of the masterpieces of the lagoon architecture.

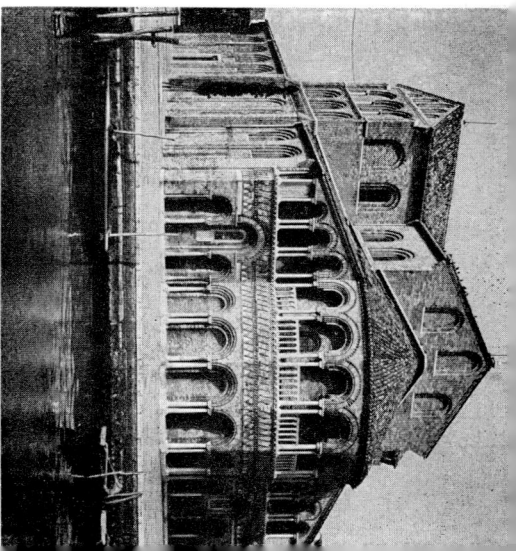

3

SAN DONATO, Murano, XII c. This is one of the oldest churches in the lagoon, having been founded in the seventh century; it was rebuilt in its present form in the twelfth century, being finished in 1140; it underwent further restoration to its original structure during the last century. The interior is in the form of a basilica, with a long high transept, and a ship's keel roof dating from the Gothic period. From the outside, the sturdy structure clearly indicates the form of the interior; the unadorned façade with double-arched pilasters is divided into three parts by the two jutting buttresses. The church was once completed by a baptistery standing in front, which was destroyed in 1719. The unadorned brickwork of the sides, with blind arches and small windows with multiple arched lintels, makes a striking contrast to the extraordinarily richly decorated apses. The apse of S. Donato takes its inspiration from St. Mark's and Santa Fosca at Torcello, which ante-date it slightly: the decoration of S. Donato is even richer and more extensive. In calls to mind the airy lightness of contemporary Veneto-byzantine secular buildings, with its blind portico with niches below, and the loggia above. Above all, the apse is still, fortunately, reflected in the water, as once were those of other churches, including, perhaps, St. Mark's itself, and, one would like to think, Santa Fosca at Torcello.

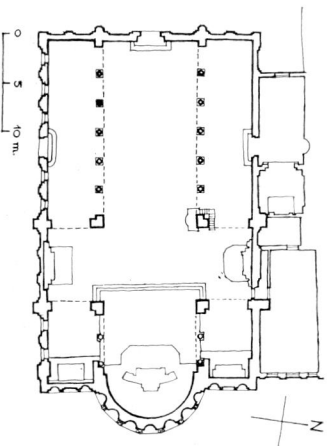

4

ST. MARK'S, XI c. The first church of St. Mark's was built in 832; a second church was erected in 978 after the fire of 976; the third church, the present one, was begun in 1063, the main structure finished in 1071, and consecrated in 1094. The church of St. Mark's has always been, right from the beginning, the Doge's chapel, and was used for civil and religious ceremonies which were part of the political life of the Republic, such as the proclamation of the Doge; it is, therefore, a part of the group of buildings of the Doge's Palace, to which it forms a magnificent appendix. Since 1807 it has been the see of the Patriarch of Venice; up to that time this had been S. Pietro di Castello. The architecture of St. Mark's, late Roman in origin, is inspired by the church of the Twelve Apostles in Constantinople, rather than that of Santa Sophia, and resembles the slightly later church of St. Front at Perigueux in France. Its plan is that of a Greek cross which is divided into three aisles by the loggia of the "matronae"; at the centre, and over each arm of the cross, stands a hemispheric cupola. These five cupolas are supported by pendentives and arches, resting on quadruple pilasters, linked to one another in their turn by arcades, loggias and a blind cupola. The apses, with their overhead cove, are subdivided below by small radial apses.

The front part of the cross, facing the square, is surrounded on three sides by the 'pronaos' or 'narthex', with apses, vaults and small cupolas. The floor inside the church is on three levels; that of the 'narthex' is on the same level as the square; the level of the floor of the aisles is raised by six steps; and that of the presbytery, which has the

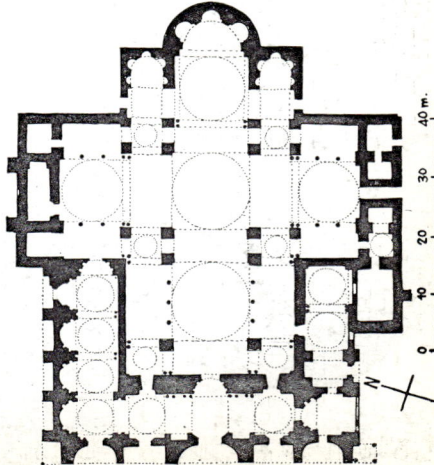

crypt below it is even higher. On the outside, the deep arches of the façades enclose between them the stout buttresses, and support the lighter arches of the loggia, with the cusps, foliage and pinnacles added in the late Gothic period. The five lead-covered cupolas are quite different in appearance seen from the outside, much higher than they appear from the inside. Built in the thirteenth century, they bear traces of oriental as well as Veneto-byzantine influence. The exterior of the central apse in brickwork,

which calls to mind Santa Fosca in Torcello, and S. Donato in Murano, is visible from the Doge's apartments. The structural and spatial complexity of St. Mark's, fruit of experience from diverse periods and countries, results in a unified whole, of exceptional strength and structural logic. Its interest is further enhanced by the rich mosaic decoration which has gradually overlaid the structure during the centuries with a highly moving effect as the unchanged witness to the life of a whole nation.

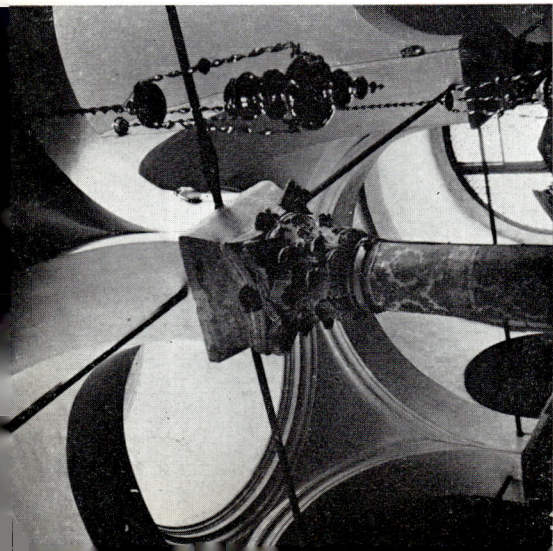

5 S. GIACOMO, Rialto, XI c.

According to tradition, this is the oldest church in Venice, dating perhaps from the fifth century. Its present form dates from the eleventh century, contemporary with the Rialto market (1097); it was partly rebuilt in 1531 and in 1601, and consequently has characteristics of various periods and styles. In its ground plan, and in its interior proportions, it is still Veneto-byzantine, a mixture of a basilical plan and a Greek cross. The oldest parts are the six Greek marble columns, with capitals and foliage, and perhaps the arches between the central and side naves. The roof dates from the sixteenth century, with barrel vaulting and a small cupola. Outside, there is the fine Gothic portico, supported by stone columns and wooden "barbacani", the only authentic example remaining in Venice, (that of San Nicolò dei Mendicoli has been rebuilt). The small campanile over the façade is baroque in style.

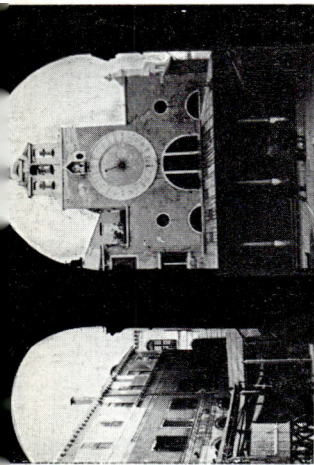

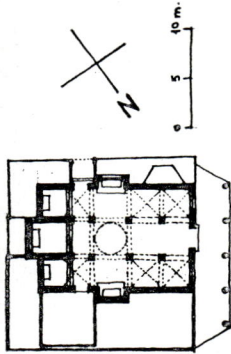

Next to the church are some small modest buildings which together make up a harmonious side to the square, and blend well with the market area.

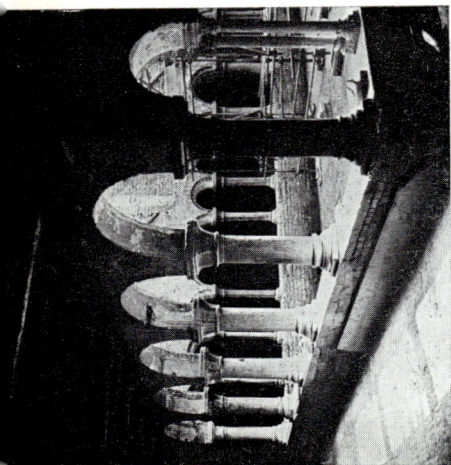

6 CLOISTER OF S. APOLLONIA, XII c.

Since 1109, together with the church of SS. Filippo e Giacomo, this cloister was part of a Benedictine monastery which depended on the famous abbey of SS. Felice e Fortunato of Ammiana, near Torcello. In 1472, the church and the monastery came under the Doge's Jurisdiction, and until 1810, the Primicerio of St. Mark's (the most important priest in the Basilica) lived here. This small cloister is a precious relic, being the only example of a Romanesque cloister in Venice. The arches surrounding the small quadrangle are irregular. The rounded arches are supported by small double columns on two of the sides and single columns on the other two. Spoiled by later additions, it has been recently restored.

7
SAN NICOLÒ DEI MENDICOLI, XII c. A very early church (perhaps dating from the seventh century, and reconstructed in the twelfth), and altered several times in successive periods.

Its Veneto-byzantine style can be seen in its basilical ground plan with three naves; dating from the same period are the small double mullioned windows of the façade, the central apse and the massive campanile. The columns and capitals of the nave, the arches of the presbytery, and the wooden-beamed ceilings of the side aisles all date from the fourteenth century gothic period.

The outside porch is also gothic in character,

having been reconstructed with the old building materials. The gilded and painted wooden wall panelling is renaissance (1580), as is the separation between the nave and the presbytery (perhaps a trace of a former iconostasis). The small side façade is a work of the transitional period between Renaissance and Baroque, while the Chapel of the Sacrament is completely Rococo. Despite the various styles imposed one upon another, or perhaps just because of this, the interior of the church has a particular charm of its own.

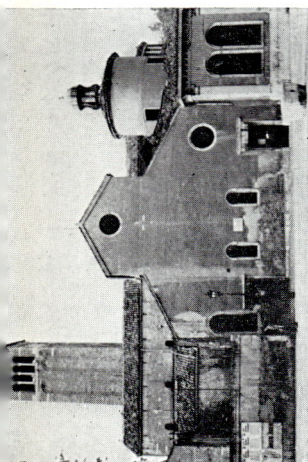

8

SAN GIACOMO DALL'ORIO, XIII s. A very early church, the first building dating from the ninth century; it was rebuilt in 1225, and subsequently underwent further alterations during the gothic period, at the beginning of the fifteenth century, and again in the sixteenth century.

Apart from the campanile, all that remains of the thirteenth century building is the ground plan, together with various pieces of the structure, and decorative elements. Its gothic feature is the sprung beam roof; the Renaissance period is to be seen especially in the apses, and in the old and new sacristies. The plan is that of a basilica with three naves and a wide transept with three naves of its own, forming almost a Greek cross, with the complex interplay of space and perspective similar to that of Santa Maria Formosa. Despite the additions and transformations undergone in various periods, the interior of this church maintains its unmistakably medieval atmosphere.

THE VENETIAN HOUSE

The Venetian house, and especially the palace, has maintained its appearance almost unchanged since the XII century, both in its interior planning and in its façades, in spite of varying styles used in the following centuries. The house was not only the residence but also commercial premises, the "fontego". For this reason on the ground floor there is a large entrance hall with a portico on the canal side for the unloading of goods, at the sides are warehouses, on the landward side a small walled courtyard, often with an outside staircase. On the mezzanine floor ("mesà") were the offices; on the main floor, "piano nobile" (of which there could be two), was the central hall ("portego") and side rooms. Above there was another floor with a lower ceiling for the servants and dependents. Like the ground plan, the façades too were divided into three parts: in the centre the loggia with filled in walls at either side, the "torreselle". Sometimes both the plan and the façade are asymmetrical, but always the façade windows correspond to the interior space division. The significance of Venetian domestic architecture is not based solely on its decorative style, as it is too often said, but on its clearly coherent and functional design.

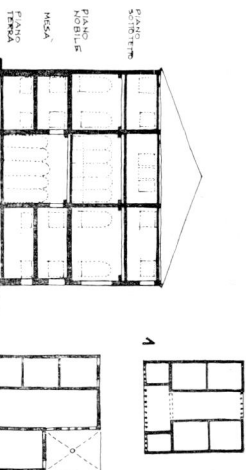

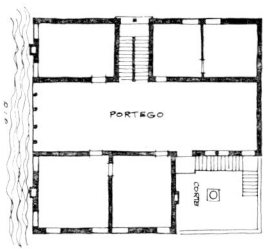

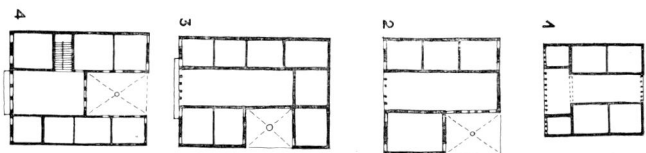

27

Plan and section of the traditional Venetian house. Other plans: 1) Byzantine tripartite, 2) « L » —, 3) « C » — and 4) « U » — shaped plans.

PIANO SOTTETTE
PIANO NOBILE
MESA
PIANO TERRA

PORTEGO
CORTE

1
2
3
4

9 CA' LOREDAN AND FARSETTI, XII c. Built in the twelfth century, the characteristics of the Veneto-byzantine palazzi can still be clearly seen, despite their having been altered, and having had storeys added above. There is the arcade on the ground floor, the open gallery running along the entire first floor, the more solid stout side areas (the torreselle), and the predominance of window space. They have kept, at least in part, their authentic appearance, which is lacking in the case of the ex Fondaco dei Turchi. Palazzo Farsetti, where Tirali built the great staircase in two flights, was the seat of the famous Accademia Farsetti during the eighteenth century, attended by Canova in his youth.

10

CA' DA MOSTO, XII c. One of the oldest palaces on the Grand Canal, and also one of the best preserved; it was built in the thirteenth century, and was the home of the famous family of navigators Da Mosto. The first two floors have the window distribution typical of houses built in the Veneto-byzantine style, with a fine loggia on the first floor. The filled-in areas at either end of the façade are decorated by small blind arches. There is more decoration above the arches of the loggia in the form of numerous "paterae", and the cornice marking the upper storey. The stilted arches of the first floor windows have pointed extradosses, thus heralding the curved arch which was to be so widely used during the Gothic period.

11

ALBERGO SALVADEGO, XV c. Building dating from the end of the thirteenth century which has kept its typical Venetian-Byzantine façade, even though it has undergone restoration. It has an unbroken series of openings on the ground floor, with small stone columns and wooden architraves; on the mezzanine floor there are arched windows. On the first floor there are high arched windows with fine central poliforas, surmounted by paterae; the top floor has a covered loggia, the 'liagò', a feature of thirteenth and fourteenth century Venetian houses: this is one of the few remaining examples. The filled-in brickwork of the central floors seems to be suspended between the two open spaces of the ground floor and the 'liagò'.

12

PALAZZETTO at the Ponte del Paradiso, XIII c. A thirteenth century construction, once belonging to the Abbey of Pomposa, showing alterations carried out during the Gothic and Renaissance periods, but, together with the houses flanking Calle del Paradiso, forms an interesting example of building and town-planning in medieval Venice. These terraced houses, modest in character, still

have the stone columns and wooden architraves of the rectangular shop windows clearly visible. They have overhanging first floors, supported by "barbacani"; which, while narrowing the space above the calle, keep the shops protected from the rain. There are two Gothic arches, one at either end of the calle: that nearest the canal is particularly fine.

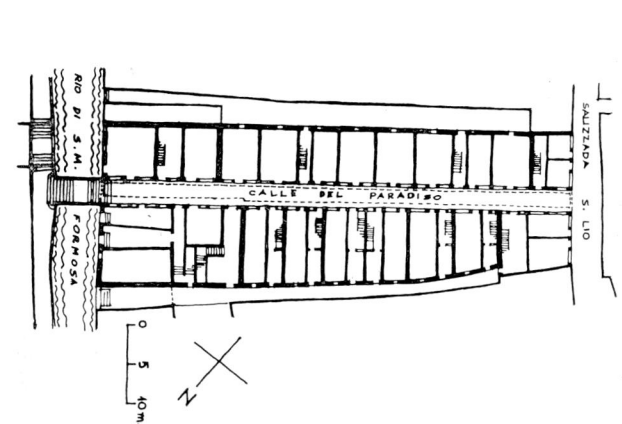

13

PALAZZETTI in Campo Santa Margherita, XIV c. These two small buildings, although belonging to different periods, have some features in common; both of them, as a whole and in their various details, have a dignified appearance, but with a slightly homely, familiar air which adds to their charm. Other features common to both buildings are the use of uncovered bricks, and the projecting roofs; the latter being rather rare in Venice, as the style was discontinued as a fire precaution, and in order to allow more light in the narrow alleys. Both the buildings have architraved openings on the ground floor, as they were intended for commercial purposes. The **left-hand house** has a fine thirteenth century doorway, and on the first floor, a series of windows of varying dimensions and styles, skilfully set in the long façade with an almost musical eurhythmy.

THE VENETIAN GOTHIC

Venetian Gothic architecture was developed from the XIV century to the middle of the XV. Flowering Gothic is a typical Venetian product. In civic architecture, while the structure of buildings remained unchanged, the Veneto-Byzantine style develops long sinuous lines in its even richer decoration and especially in the marble fretwork which has the grace and elegance of lace. In religious architecture the Ravenna type of church is linked with the new forms and needs of the monastic orders. We thus have the great churches of Frari and of St. John and St. Paul and those of S. Stefano and Madonna dell'Orto, where Gothic arches and ribbed vaults are reinforced by tie-beams and wooden brackets in the ancient local tradition. These churches have a simple and open appearance which is quite different from the original Northern Gothic.

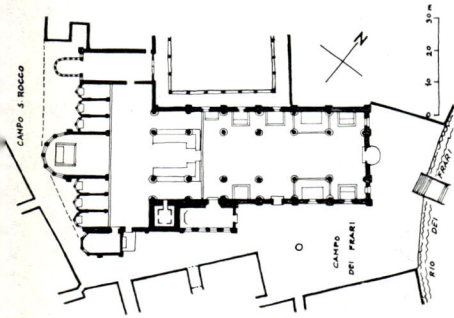

14
SANTA MARIA GLORIOSA DEI FRARI XIV c. Built by the minor friars of St. Francis, the "Frari", it is one of the most important churches in the city; it came to be known as "Ca' Grande", being one of the most outstanding examples of Venetian Gothic. Formerly on this site stood a smaller church, begun in 1250, and finished in 1338, with its apses facing the canal where the present-day façade now stands. The work on the apses of the new church was begun in 1340; it was finished in 1443, the old church having been meanwhile demolished in 1415, and the new church was consecrated in 1469. The plan is attributed to Friar Scipione Bon, whose richly decorated tomb stands in the church. The building is in the form of a Latin cross, with three aisles and a small

transept with the apse chapels leading off, a central one and six lateral chapels, on a polygonal plan; they make up an interesting group when seen from Campo San Rocco. To the North of the church stands the Sacristy, with the Pesaro chapel, and the imposing cloisters, and around these, the huge old convent, which, since the eighteenth century, has housed the famous Venetian State Archives, some of the most important in the world. To the South are the Corner and Emiliani chapels, as well as the massive bell tower (1361-96). The severe façade has a curved crowning, divided into three parts by stout pilasters: the cornice is decorated by small tabernacles, and by curved crowning which was placed above the original profile of the roof, perhaps in an attempt to rival the height of the church of S. John and St. Paul. The interior of the church, with its twelve columns, the cross vaulted roof, with its characteristic wooden tie-beams, is magnificently effective. The three naves merge into a large single unit of space. They are protracted longitudinally due to the joining of the two naves into which the church was divided; the public area for services and preaching and the area for the Convent use, its level raised by two steps, more articulated, richly decorated, and better lit. This part includes the Choir, the transept, the apse chapels, communicating through the Sacristy with the Convent cloisters. The Choir in front of the altar is the only remaining example of its kind (1475). Here are to be found many precious masterpieces of painting and sculpture by Giovanni Bellini, Vivarini, Lombardo, Donatello, Rizzo, Sansovino, Vittoria, Canova together with Tiziano's famous Assumption over the High Altar.

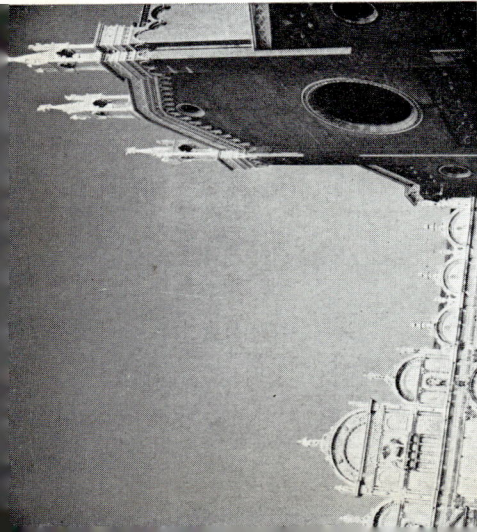

CAMPO S. S. GIOVANNI E PAOLO

15
CHURCH OF ST. JOHN AND ST. PAUL, XIV c. Built by Domenican Friars, this is the second largest Gothic church of Venice, almost as vast as the Frari church. The building was begun halfway through the fourteenth century: the apses and transept had been completed by 1368, and the church was consecrated in 1430. It is built on a basilica plan with three naves and a transept and five apse chapels; other chapels dedicated to St. Philip, to the Madonna Addolorata, and to St. Dominic, have been added on the south side, while on the north side, beyond the Rosary chapel, lies the cloister of the convent. The tall unadorned façade, in striking contrast with the extremely ornate façade of the School of St. Mark, has a sloping outline, and is only adorned at the top by the small hanging arcades and by the three tabernacles. The doorway, with columns salvaged from Torcello, was to have been the beginning of a new façade, begun in the second half of the fifteenth century by Antonio Gambello. The side view, marked out by pilasters, forms a complex structure, with side chapels, transept, and the cupola added at a later date. The articulation of masses continues at the back with the fine apses, and small structures like the ex-School of St. Ursula. The interior is cross-vaulted, with wooden tie-beams as in the Frari church, supported by ten massive columns, two of them tri-lobate. Up to 1682 there existed here too a wooden choir in the middle of the central nave. The presbytery, the side chapels and the transept, on a higher level than the main nave, are all lit by large ornate windows which give a particularly luminous atmosphere to the whole of this part of the church. This Venetian Pantheon is enriched by funeral monuments and works of art of varying periods, by some of the greatest artists working in Venice.

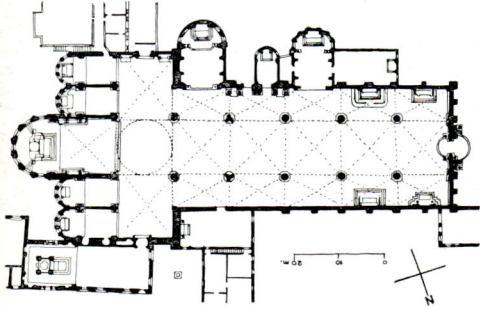

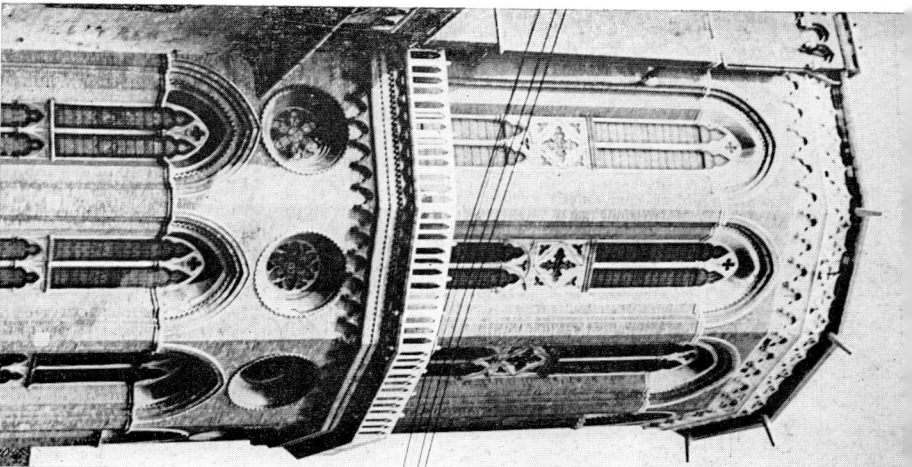

16
**SANTO STEFANO, Cloister and Church,
XIV c.** Conventual church of the Augustinian
order which was rebuilt halfway through the
fourteenth century (completed in 1374), on
the site of an earlier thirteenth century church,
and had a decorated Gothic **portal** (a) added
at the beginning of the fifteenth century by
Bartolomeo Bon. The interior, agreeably well-

lit, has three naves separated by high wide
arches, and a beautiful sprung-beam **roof** (b),
one of the best examples of this type. In
the middle of the nave, as in the Frari
church, once stood the choir, now placed
behind the altar. Both in the church and in
the sacristy there is a valuable collection
of works of art by Vivarini, Tintoretto, Palma,

Pietro Lombardo, Vittoria, Canova, etc., besides the tomb of the famous musician Gabrieli.
Adjoining the church is the Augustinian
convent (1532) attributed to Scarpagnino; the
cloister (c) of a solemn dignified appearance,
was decorated on the courtyard side by
frescoes by Pordenone, now almost entirely
obliterated.

17

MADONNA DELL'ORTO, Church and Cloister, XIV c. This charming church was built in the middle of the fourteenth century by Fra Tiberio of Parma, and altered in the fifteenth century. The richly decorated façade is one of the best preserved examples of Venetian Gothic; elements of various periods are combined together, resulting in architecture of great dignity, despite its surprisingly modest dimensions. The two stout central pilasters, almost buttresses, give the façade verticality;

the slanting rows of niches, Romanesque in origin, are superimposed on the original simple structure, thereby enriching it considerably. The two fine side-windows and the doorway are late Gothic, the latter already showing signs of the Renaissance. The many statues on the façade are very finely carved. The unusual campanile, with its onion-shaped cupola, has an oriental air. The interior is extremely simple, with three naves and a flat roof which was probably originally sprung-

beam (ship's keel), like that of Santo Stefano; the apses, too, are similar. The church is decorated by several **paintings** (b) of Tintoretto in their original positions. Amongst other works of art, there is a fine Madonna by Bellini, and a splendid Cima da Conegliano. Adjoining the church is the old Gothic **cloister,** now completely neglected, and in the **Campo** stands the **Scuola dei Mercanti** dating from the sixteenth century, based on plans of Palladio.

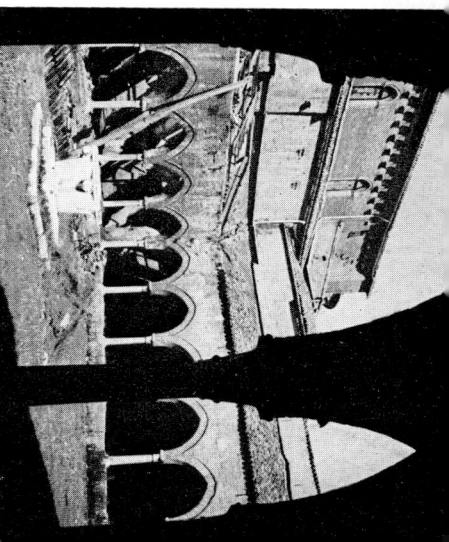

18
SANT'ELENA, Church and Cloister, XV c.
The monastery of the Olivetan monks was at one time isolated in the middle of the lagoon, and in the thirteenth century, the body of Sant'Elena was brought there. The church, rebuilt in 1435, has a single nave, tall and narrow like the façade. Its unusual proportions are balanced by the side extension formed by the large chapels of Sant'Elena and San Giustinian on the right, and that of Santa Romana on the left. The exterior is particularly fine, the façade being enriched by the famous monumental doorway dedicated to Vittore Cappello by Antonio Rizzo, and given a sense of movement at the side and at the back by the elaborate chapels and apses facing the lagoon. To the left is the fifteenth century cloister, now reduced to only three sides, with the light architraved arcade facing the church.

19

S. GIOVANNI IN BRAGORA, XV c. The church was founded perhaps in the eighth century, and altered in the ninth and twelfth centuries; it was rebuilt in 1475 in the Gothic style and completed towards the end of the fifteenth century by the Renaissance presbytery. The façade has curved crowning, Gothic in its inspiration, but already approaching the style of Coducci. The interior has three naves, the central one has very old columns and a sprung beam roof: it once had the choir in the middle, and the seven marble pieces remaining from it are now in the presbytery. Other relics of the older buildings are the sacristy door, and perhaps the small circular apse near the entrance. The church, which has a modest, informal appearance, full of charm, contains priceless works of art, such as the splendid painting of Cima da Conegliano, and features of historical interest, such as the font where Vivaldi was baptised, and the tomb of the architect Massari.

20

S. GREGORIO, Church and Abbey, XV c.
The church, founded in 806 and in 989 given to the Benedictine monks, was rebuilt in its present form in the middle of the fifteenth century. The apses were added later in 1461. It is closely modelled on the church of the Carità, which antedates it slightly, both in its plan, its façade and its apses; those of San Gregorio are some of the few which can still be seen reflected in the waters of a canal, thereby emphasising the vertical elegance. The tiny cloister adjoining the church, with its charming façade on the Grand Canal, is the only remaining piece of the large Benedictine monastery founded in 1160, where the monks of Sant'Ilario were transferred in 1214.

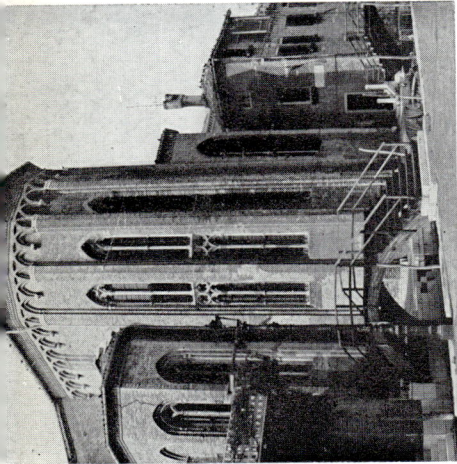

21

SANT'ALVISE, XIV c. A conventual church, built in 1388. The façade, divided by slightly protruding pilasters, with hanging arches, and with its small pointed doorway, was raised at the sides, perhaps in the seventeenth century, in order to build the interior flat ceiling, still shows signs of being a monastic building. The small **campanile** (b) too, with cusp and corner towers, is in keeping with this character. Inside the church, restored in the seventeenth century, is to be seen the **barco** (c), a singing gallery for nuns, one of the earliest of its kind, with fine eighteenth century wrought-iron grilles. Besides the two paintings of Tiepolo, the eight fifteenth-century panels in tempera are worthy of notice, attributed by Ruskin to Carpaccio.

b

22
MISERICORDIA, Church, Abbey and Scuola Vecchia, XIV c. This ancient church, founded in the tenth century, once known as Santa Maria di Valverde, had its façade rebuilt in the baroque style in 1659. Nearby is the Scuola Vecchia della Misericordia, founded in 1303, a delightful Gothic building with its elegant façade crowned by a curved top, pinnacles at either side, and two large windows with iron gratings.
The richly decorated doorway, with canopy,

had a large lunette framing a piece of sculpture by Bartolomeo Bon, pulled down in 1612. Fragments of this are to be seen in the Victoria and Albert Museum in London. The side along the canal is of particular interest with pilasters and a jutting cornice. The portico, opened in 1503, modernises the ancient building from a town-planning point of view. Between the church and the Scuola there is a cloister, a relic of the original abbey.

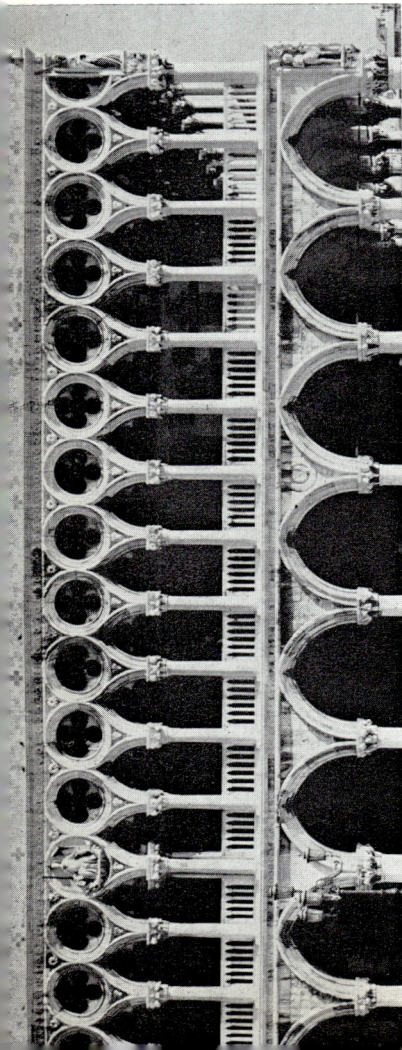

23
DOGE'S PALACE (Gothic part), XIV c.

The first palace was built in the ninth century, when the Doges transferred their headquarters here from Malamocco; it was built in the form of a stout castle, as can be deduced from the massive walls remaining, which now form part of the Treasury of St. Mark's and of the Foscari Arch. The palace was enlarged and rebuilt several times during the twelfth century, until the rebuilding carried out by Doge Ziani which gave the Piazzetta and the Piazza their present form. The appearance of the twelfth century building must have been similar to Veneto-byzantine buildings of the same period, with portico and loggias. The Hall of the Maggior Consiglio was rebuilt between 1340 and 1365, renovating the whole wing overlooking the waterfront; this façade can be said to have been finished in 1419 in its present form. The central window of

the Delle Masegne brothers dates from 1404. In 1424 the extension of the palace in the same style towards the Piazzetta as well was carried out, the previous Veneto-byzantine building having been demolished. The Gothic part was finished near the church by the richly decorated Porta della Carta (1438-1441), the work of the Bon family, and by the Foscari arch which was built between 1462 and 1471. The designer of the palace, built by Tuscan workmen with the Lamberti family, Lombard workmen under Matteo Raverti, and Venetians under the Bon father and son, is unknown. The seventeen arches of the portico overlooking the waterfront, and the eighteen overlooking the Piazzetta, support the uninterrupted loggia with double the number of arches, and the quadrilobate cross traceries with their deep openings, for a length of 71,5 by 75 metres; above this is the filled-in

wall with the fourteen large windows. The harmonious development of the façade is inspired by the Veneto-byzantine architecture in the succession of loggias, and in the spacious way the building opens out towards the exterior, and by the religious architecture of the central aisles of Gothic churches in the inversion of spaces and solids, and by the entire experience of Gothic and Oriental art in the rich plastic decoration and in the polychrome wall-covering. The portico and the loggia of the palace, together with the other buildings surrounding the Piazza, make up a single architectural composition from a town-planning point of view. Thus the traditional Greek and Roman plan of open spaces, and of squares surrounded by porticos was revived.

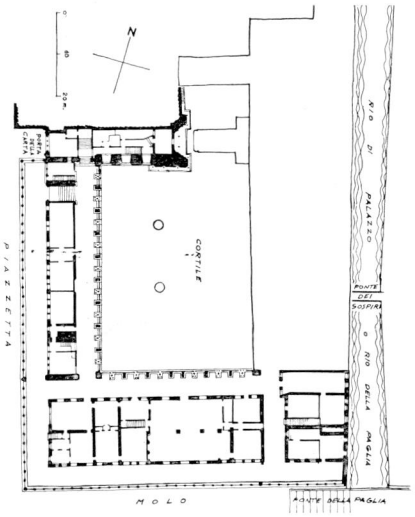

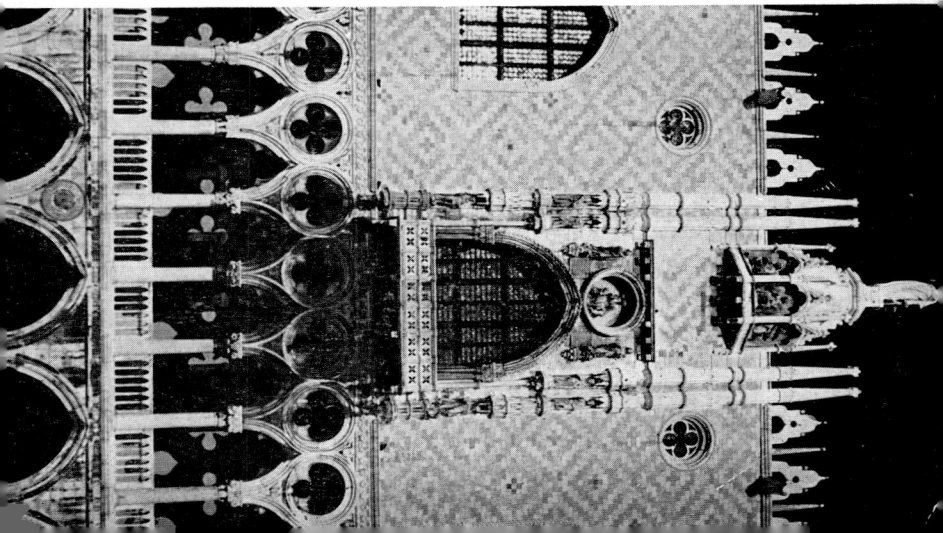

24

PAL. ARIANI-MINOTTO, XIII c. Built in the second half of the fourteenth century; the features dating from this period are the first floor windows, particularly the fenestration with the pierced stone screens above the arches, oriental in character, but later developed into fifteenth century Gothic windows. The asymmetry of the façade, directly linked to the interior distribution of the rooms, the small portico on the corner with the open air staircase, together with the free introduction of motifs of later periods, are all typical features of secular Venetian architecture during the Middle Ages.

25

CA' FOSCARI AND PALAZZI GIUSTINIAN, XV c. The façades of these palaces make up one of the best examples of fifteenth century Gothic along the Grand Canal. Ca' Foscari, to the right, shows the final stage of the development of the "tower-house", its verticality minimised by the superimposed open galleries. The Giustinian palazzi, to the left, are conceived horizontally, two almost identical buildings being joined together. Both possess central open galleries on the "piano nobile", surmounted by quadrilobate crossed tracery as in the loggia of the Ducal Palace.

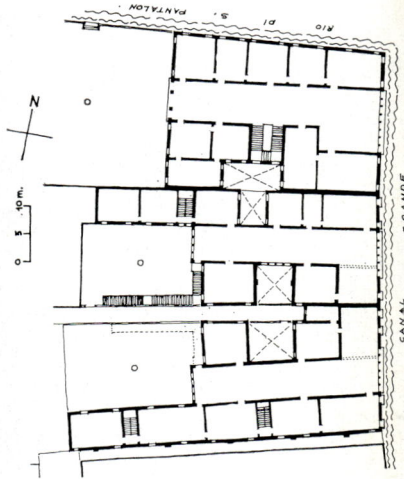

42

26

CA' D'ORO, XV c. Designed by Marco d'Amadio and carried out and decorated by first Lombard and later Venetian stonemasons, supervised by Matteo Reverti and Giovanni and Bartolomeo Bon, this building was completed in 1434. A gem of Venetian decorated Gothic architecture, the Ca' d'Oro embodies with exquisite taste the later trends and solutions from the Veneto-Byzantine to the decorated Gothic styles. Apart from the well-known beauty of its façade, like an Oriental carpet, its structural coherence should be noted. Its asymmetrical design is not accidental, but is derived from earlier buildings

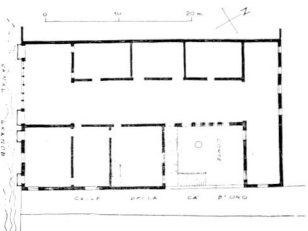

(e.g. Palazzo Ariani Minotto), and clearly shows how the rooms are arranged inside and their various functions. The stone tracery too of the portico and the loggias follow the logic of statics, transforming it into a design, progressively diminishing the dimensions and thickness of columns, arches, tracery etc. from the base to the top. The articulation of interior space, on the ground floor with courtyard entrance and portico, on the upper floors with large room and loggia, is resolved in varied, complex ways.

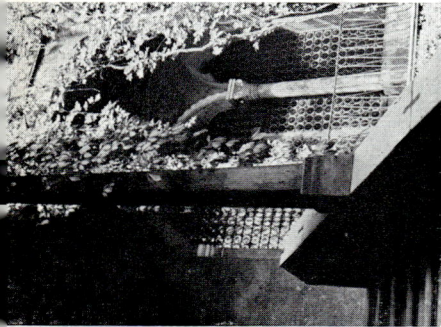

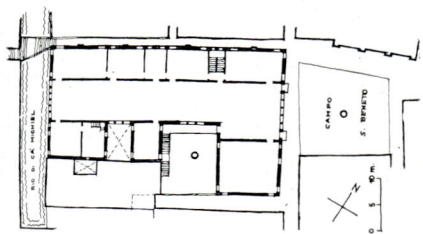

27
PALAZZO FORTUNY or "degli Orfei" at San Beneto, XV c. A colossal, almost isolated building (most unusual in Venice), in fifteenth century Venetian Gothic style; the ground-plan is almost square with a small side courtyard, where an open-air arcaded stair-case is situated. The two façades, one domi-nating the Campo, and the other overlooking the canal are quite different in character: the former is more richly decorated and open, and the other one is more severe and sober. Despite the Venetian Gothic decora-tions, the palazzo has something of the harsh appearance of a castle; its charm lies in its authenticity which has been preserved by recent intelligent restorations.

28
PALAZZO CENTANI (Goldoni's House), XV c. This house, famous because Carlo Goldoni was born here in 1707, now houses the Institute of Theatrical Studies. It is a typical Venetian-Gothic construction with a curved façade which follows the bend of the canal it overlooks. The two upper storeys, which are the best preserved, have the centre

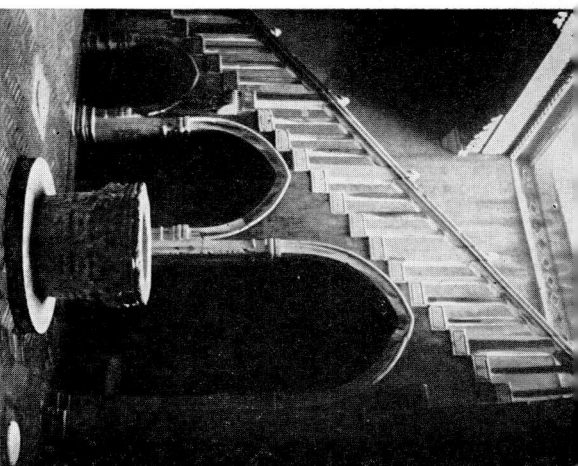

windows and the side windows spaced asymmetrically; to the right, the large chimney is clearly visible. The most attractive part of the house is the courtyard, which is extremely picturesque, with its traditional open-air stairway, one of the few examples which is roofed in. It is not a sumptuous house, but one full of a simple dignity.

29
PALAZZO GIOVANELLI at San Felice, XV c.
A magnificent fifteenth century aristocratic house in late Gothic style, once famous for the entertainments given here in the sixteenth and eighteenth centuries, and for its splendid art collection, which included Giorgione's « Tempest ». The enormous size of the building, with its massive lower floors, is lightened

in the upper floors by the central loggia with quadrilobate openwork above the arches, and especially by the mullioned corner window, one of the most decorated examples of its kind. Inside, the neo-Gothic **staircase,** constructed in the nineteenth century by G.B. Meduna, already heralds the fashion for art nouveau.

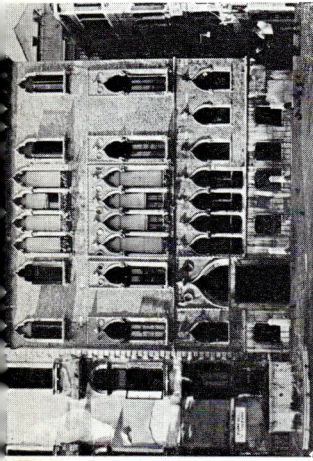

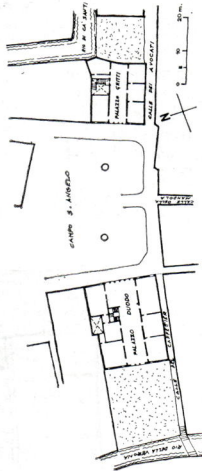

30

PALAZZO PRIULI San Provolo, XV c. An imposing aristocratic house dating from the first half of the fifteenth century with characteristic harmonious central windows. The two corner mullioned windows are of great interest from a static, as well as a decorative point of view; of the two, the left-hand one is particularly well decorated. At the back, facing Campo San Severo, the portal of the street entrance testifies to the magnificence of the whole; the façade was once decorated by frescoes which have since vanished, painted by Palma il Vecchio at the beginning of the sixteenth century.

31

CAMPO S. ANGELO, Palazzi Duodo and Gritti, XV c. Two beautiful Gothic buildings remain in Campo S. Angelo, Palazzo Duodo and Palazzo Gritti, facing each other across the campo. Though dating from the same period, the XVth century, they are quite different in appearance. **Palazzo Duodo** (b) shows clearly the traditional characteristics of an aristocratic residence: the ground and mezzanine floors, intended for use as storerooms, have only those very narrow windows which were strictly necessary; the first floor (piano nobile) has much larger rooms and, on the façade, an almost unbroken series of windows. **Palazzo Gritti** (a) has the ground floor reduced to the minimum height, thus making the mezzanine floor, with its central mullioned window, into a kind of third « piano nobile ». Compared with that of Palazzo Duodo, the façade of Palazzo Gritti has a vertical rhythm, and reveals a refinement of taste in decoration which already heralds the Renaissance style (see Palazzo Dario no. 34).

THE RENAISSANCE IN VENICE

The Renaissance style was adopted rather later in Venetian architecture than it was in other regions in Italy: it first appeared well on in the fifteenth century and was established towards the end of the century. The Renaissance style was introduced in Venice by Tuscan architects, like Michelozzo on the Island of S. Giorgio and, later on, by Rossellino at S. Giobbe, and by sculptors and stone masons such as Jacopo della Quercia and the Lamberti family in the Doge's Palace and Andrea Verrocchio at St. John and St. Paul. However it fell to Lombard architects and stone masons to bring to Venice the style which originated in Tuscany: Piero Lombardo, who had been to Florence, and Mauro Coducci who revived the forms and designs of Leon Battista Alberti. The work of the Lombardo family, of Coducci and, later on, Rizzo, gave Venetian Renaissance architecture a character of its own, going back to the decorative style, chromatic taste and to the constructional ideas of the old Veneto-byzantine tradition. Towards the end of the fifteenth century a golden age began in Venice for all art forms. « Seldom in the history of European art — says Hugh Honour with reason — have painters, sculptors and architects worked in such close harmony as in early Renaissance Venice... The Lombardo family occupies a position of capital importance, for they invented the style of architecture and sculpture which is depicted in so many paintings by Giovanni Bellini and his contemporaries ».

32
THE ARSENAL, Archway, 1460. The Great Archway, built by Gambello in 1460, is considered to be the first example of Renaissance architecture in Venice. It is however, actually composed of some parts of older buildings, such as the four Greek marble columns, with their Byzantine capitals, the foliage-covered cornices of the arch, and of the entablature etc. After the victorious naval battle of Lepanto (1571), it was embellished by two commemorative statues, and in 1682 a terrace was built in front of it, to replace a bridge (probably a draw-bridge).
Close to land entrance is the water entrance from Canal delle Galleazze, defended by the stout sixteenth century towers (1574). The enormous walls and towers, which jealously guarded the themselves a striking piece of architecture, area of the Arsenal, constitute in and a characteristic part of Venice.

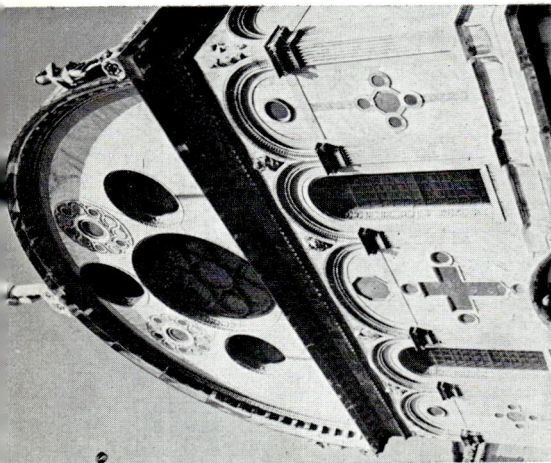

33
SPIRAL STAIRCASE, Palazzo Contarini, XV c.
This is the earliest and most famous example of a spiral staircase in Venice; built at the end of the fifteenth century, the staircase has a Renaissance air, but still shows some Gothic elements in the capitals, in the stairs, in the arches of the loggias, etc. The uninterrupted succession of arches, both in the spiral staircase and in the loggias, gives the building a lightness which recalls the Ravenna type of bell-towers, such as those of Tessera and Caorle.

34
PALAZZO DARIO on the Grand Canal, 1487.
A delightful Renaissance house, built in 1487 by one of the Lombardo family (perhaps Pietro) for Giovanni Dario who was secretary to the Republic in Constantinople. The building follows the Venetian tradition in the layout of the rooms and in the asymmetry of the façade; the new style of the Renaissance is intermingled with the classical outlines, in the shape of the arches, and in the geometrical decoration; the polychrome marbles, and the interlacing designs give the building a richness which is oriental in its effect. It is an elegant piece of secular architecture to be compared to the Miracoli church.

35
SANTA MARIA DEI MIRACOLI, P. Lombardo, 1481 - 89. The church was built between 1481-1489 from a design by Pietro Lombardo, who was helped in the work by his sons. He also built the nearby monastery, which was formerly connected to the church by means of an overhead gallery. This small building is isolated from the surrounding houses, by a canal on one side, and a calle on the other, and its surface is entirely covered, both inside and out, by architectural

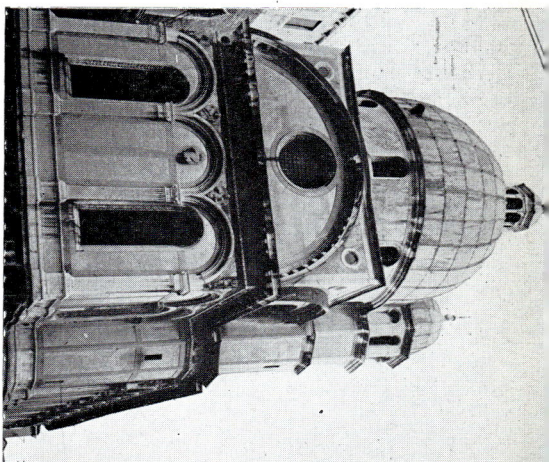

divisions, inlaid polychrome marbles, bas-reliefs and statues. The interior has a single nave, a wooden barrel-vaulted ceiling, and the 'barco' (choir gallery for nuns) above the main doorway. The Presbytery, on a raised level, is covered by a small cupola. The richness of the decoration, the elegance of line and of architectural proportions, the artistic unity of the building, both in its design and construction, make this church a jewel of the Renaissance art of Venice.

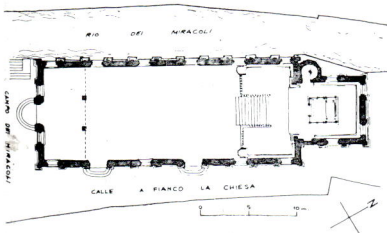

36

S. GIOBBE, P. Lombardo, 1470. In the XIVth century a small oratory existed on this site, adjoining an almshouse founded in 1378. Half-way through the XVth century, the church was rebuilt with a contribution from Doge Cristoforo Moro, on a design by Antonio Gambello. Of this early Gothic church there remain some double windows on the south side, the exterior pilasters of the apse, the ante-sacristy and the bell-tower. Dating from the same period is the remaining wing of the cloister, with the portico and chapter house. The church was transformed in 1470, and at the beginning of the XVIth century by Pietro Lombardo, who executed here one of the earliest examples of Renaissance architecture in Venice. It is, above all, remarkable for some details of great constructive and decorative value, such as the main doorway of the façade, the two small side chapels (1502-6), and on the left the chapel of St. Luke (beginning of the sixteenth century). On the left side, too, is a rare example of Tuscan workmanship, the chapel of the Martini family, silk weavers originally from Lucca, probably designed by Antonio Rossellino, who was also responsible for the sculptures on the altar, the vault of which is decorated by polychrome terra-cottas by the Della Robbia family. The deep choir, with its late XVIth century choirstalls, is reminiscent of Palladio's in San Giorgio. The paintings and sculpture of the same period are worthy of note.

37
PALAZZO GUSSONI at San Lio, P. Lombardo, late XV c. Once Gothic in style, this delightful house was rebuilt towards the end of the fifteenth century by Pietro Lombardo. The elaborately decorated façade facing the canal, with its daring asymmetry, is one of the most successful examples of the elegant Lombard style in civic architecture of the early Renaissance. This façade, however, is only the final development of the interesting interior of the building, round a tiny courtyard; with small portico and entrance hall on the ground floor, the hall and other rooms on the first floor, all designed and arranged with great skill.

38
PAL. MALIPIERO TREVISAN. Santa Maria Formosa, early XVI c. A building dating from the first half of the sixteenth century, attributed to Sante Lombardo, this is one of the most elegant aristocratic homes of the period. The façade, divided into three parts, with the central windows and solid walls at the sides in the ancient tradition, is here marked by the continuous line of the horizontal cornices. Even though the building overlooks the canal, the white façade constitutes an integral part of the urban composition of Campo Santa Maria Formosa.

MAURO CODUCCI

Mauro Coducci (born Lenna, Bergamo, 1440 - died Venice 1504) is held to be the greatest early Renaissance architect in Venice, where he worked from 1469, almost at the same time as the Lombardo family. Coducci, too, used Tuscan elements, particularly those of Leon Battista Alberti (e.g. curved crowning on church façades, arched double windows and rusticated basements for palaces). He also goes back to the Byzantine tradition, as in the Procuratie arches and in the Greek cross plan of S. Giovanni Grisostomo. Compared with his rivals, the Lombardo family, Coducci shows a clearer grasp of constructional and, especially, spatial ideas, without allowing decoration for its own sake. In religious architecture, besides the exquisite S. Michele, and the monumental S. Zaccaria, Coducci built that masterpiece of spatial clarity S. Maria Formosa and the small church of San Giovanni Grisostomo above mentioned. In the field of secular architecture, the Procuratie and the Clok Tower are perfectly coherent with Coducci's cultural background, while in the Zorzi Palace at S. Severo and Corner-Spinelli and Vendramin-Calergi Palaces on the Grand Canal, the architect shows us the possibilities of the new style in a typically Venetian setting.

39

SCHOOL OF ST. JOHN THE EVANGELIST, 1349-1512. This is another of the 'Scuole Grandi' (Great Guilds), founded in 1349. The building was reconstructed halfway through the fifteenth century, in the Decorated Gothic style; the side façade (1454) and the ground floor hall both date from this period. The building was completed in the Renaissance era with the lovely exterior marble screen, designed by Pietro Lombardo in 1481. The interior stairway with two flights (1498), and

the Doorway (1512), are both the work of Mauro Coducci. The Hall on the first floor was redesigned in 1727 by Giorgio Massari. Apart from Coducci's imposing stairway, unique of its kind, the most interesting part of the building is the courtyard, where, despite differing architectural styles, and the work of several architects, a characteristic corner of the city has been created — one of the most delighful and interesting in the whole of Venice.

40
SCHOOL OF ST. MARK'S (now Civic Hospital), 1487-1530. This was one of the six 'Scuole Grandi' (Great Guilds) of Venice, founded in 1260. The present building, which was constructed between 1487 and 1490 to replace an earlier one which was almost entirely destroyed by fire in 1485, was designed by Pietro Lombardo helped by his sons and Antonio Buora in the work. The curved crowning of the façade was completed by

Mauro Coducci in 1495. The building was enlarged at the back by Jacopo Sansovino between 1533 and 1546. The façade, elaborately decorated, is divided into two parts vertically, each of which is subdivided into three parts by fluted pilasters. The left-hand part, with the main doorway, corresponds to the Entrance Hall and the Great Hall on the floor above, and is the more imposing. The right-hand part corresponds to the side

rooms, and is more modestly decorated. Together, they make up the asymmetrical façade, which is naturally joined to the church of St. John and St. Paul. The side of the Scuola, which overlooks the Rio dei Mendicanti, is stressed by elegant pilasters, and by the corresponding jutting cornice. The interior dimensions, especially the Entrance Hall and the Stairway, have a magnificence and dignity all their own.

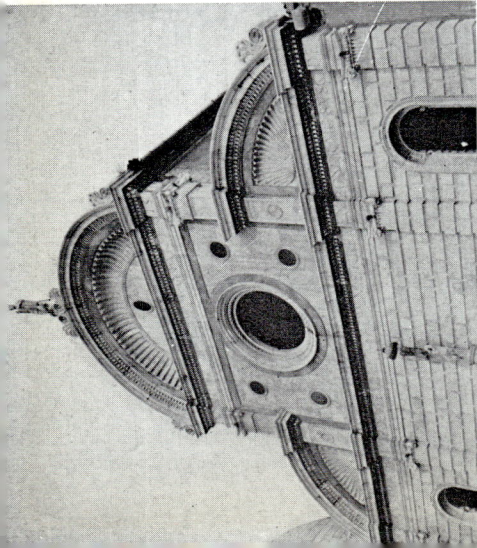

a

41
S. MICHELE IN ISOLA, Mauro Coducci, 1496.
There seems to have been a small tenth-century church dedicated to St. Michele on the island, where St. Romualdo, founder of the Camaldolese Order, is supposed to have lived. The island belonged to this order from 1212 until the beginning of the XIXth century, when they were transferred to Rome. In this famous abbey, among the many learned men who lived here, was Fra Mauro († 1459) author of the first planisphere, now preserved in the Marciana Library. After having been used as a prison, from 1837 onwards, the island became the municipal cemetery. The church is the earliest religious Renaissance building in Venice; it was built by Coducci in 1469. The façade, with its simple, harmonious architectural lines, is the first example of triple curved crowning, a theme which was to be repeated in a more elaborate form in the façade of S. Zaccaria. The interior, too, is particularly graceful, and is divided into two parts by the barco, or hanging choir gallery for monks. From the vestibule, passing underneath the choir, one enters the church proper, with three naves, apse and side-chapels, a succession of areas which are particularly interesting. Adjoining the church is the Emiliana chapel, an elegant hexagonal building designed by Guglielmo Bergamasco (1530). The fine campanile is Gothic in style, as are the peaceful fifteenth century cloisters.

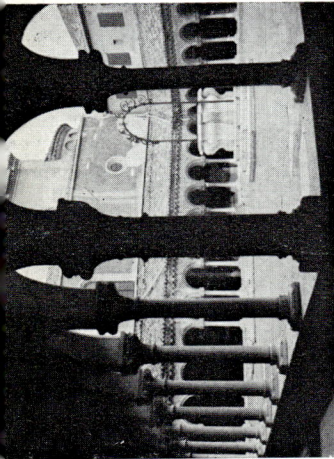

42
SAN ZACCARIA, XV c. In this church, founded in the ninth century, and the adjoining convent of the Benedictine nuns, there are still traces of the original building, where eight of the first Doges were buried. The original construction can be seen in the crypt underneath the chapel of St. Tarasio; this formed the central apse of the second church or 'chiesa vecchia' built in the Gothic period (1444-65), and was intended for the use of the nuns. Part of the central nave can still be seen, together with the façade, to

54

the right of the present imposing Renaissance church, which is therefore the third successive building. This was begun in the Gothic style by Antonio Gambello between 1458 and 1481, and was continued in the Renaissance style by Mauro Coducci from 1480 to 1500, being finally completed in 1515. On Easter day the Doge used to make an official visit to the church, which was used for ceremonial rather than conventual purposes. The plan is Gothic in style: the **ambulatory** (c) with four radial chapels is the only example of its kind in Venice, and one of the few in Italy. In the Renaissance style are the spacious arcades of the interior, and the upper part of the magnificent **façade** (a) which is considered to be Coducci's masterpiece. Among the memorable works of art preserved in the church are the frescoes of Andrea del Castagno (1442), and the three fifteenth-century polyptychs in the apse of the old church (chapel of St. Tarasio) and the famous altarpiece by Giovanni Bellini (1505). There is also a fine old square bell-tower of the thirteenth century, the sixteenth century cloisters of the convent (now used as a barracks) which are linked to the church by means of an open loggia behind the **apses** (d).

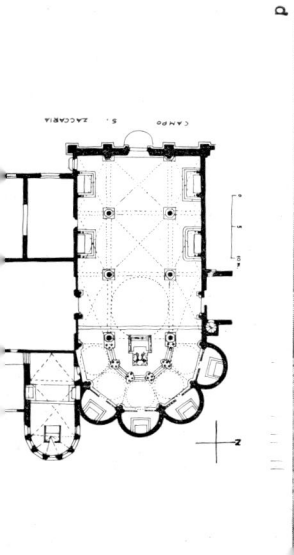

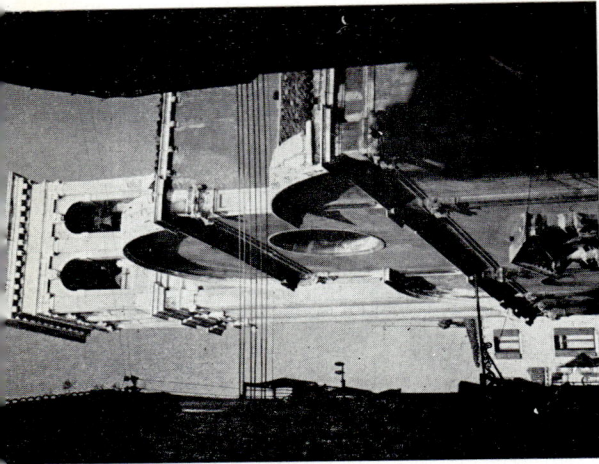

43
SANTA MARIA FORMOSA, Mauro Coducci, 1942. According to tradition, the original church was built in the seventh century, rebuilt in the eleventh, and finally reconstructed in 1492 by Mauro Coducci. The Greek Cross plan of the present church was perhaps inspired by St. Mark's; this kind of plan was dear to Coducci who was to use it also in the church of St. John Grisostomo. The setting of the church, and of the bell tower (1611-1688) with regard to the Campo and the canals, also the plan and dimensions of the apses, has much in common with San Giacomo dall'Orio. The interior, with its simple, essential lines, has an articulation and a complexity rare in Renaissance architecture. The two façades date from later periods: that facing the canal (1542) is of the Sansovino school, and that facing the Campo from 1604. Amongst the works of art in the church the triptych of Bernardo Vivarini (1473) and the St. Barbara by Palma il Vecchio (1509) are particularly worthy of note.

44
SAN GIOVANNI GRISOSTOMO, M. Coducci, 1497-1504. This is the last work of Mauro Coducci, built between 1497 and 1504, the decoration being finished later in 1525. The façade, with its curved crowning recalls other churches built by Coducci. It is built on a Greek cross plan, inscribed within a square; a design beloved of the fifteenth century theorists, and going back

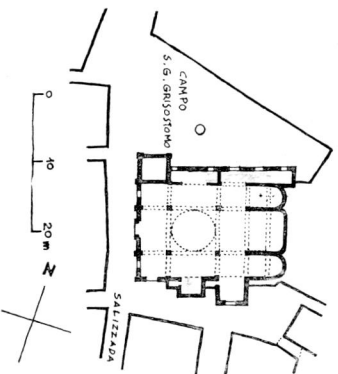

originally to Byzantine origins. In the centre is the dome, supported by pillars and arches, and between the arms of the cross, with their dome vaulting, are the four corners, also with domes. The architectural whole is of an exemplary clarity and coherence; the interior space is clearly indicated by the exterior architecture, despite the additions. Next to the church is the bell tower, built between 1530 and 1590. Amongst the many works of art inside the church, are the panels of Giovanni Bellini (1513), and those of Sebastian del Piombo (1508-1511), and the marble panel of Tullio Lombardo (1500-1502); these are particularly worthy of note because they originate in the same period, and are in the same style as the architecture of the church itself.

45
PROCURATIE VECCHIE and Clock Tower, M. Coducci, 1500-32. The Procuratie Vecchie, which occupy the whole of the North side of the Piazza, were built by Mauro Coducci as far as the first order of loggias in 1500; the building was continued after 1512 by Bartolomeo Bon and Guglielmo dei Grigi, and was completed at the far end of the Piazza by Jacopo Sansovino in 1532. The succession of the 50 arches of the portico, and the double arches of the two loggias, were based on the former Veneto-Byzantine building, repeating with Renaissance elegance the lightness, the rhythm, and the graceful open proportions

of the earlier building.
The Clock Tower, too, was based on designs by Mauro Coducci, and built between 1496 and 1499. The two side wings were added by Pietro Lombardo between 1500-1506, and later still, additional floors by Giorgio Massari in 1755. The elegant architecture, which acts as a background to the Piazzetta, is completed by the famous figures of the 'Moors' with the great Bell (1497) at the top of the tower, and on the front by the coloured enamels and gold decoration. Both these features are Renaissance interpretations of traditional Veneto-Byzantine style decorations.

46

PALAZZO ZORZI at S. Severo, Mauro Coducci, 1500. This elegant Renaissance palace was built by Mauro Coducci at the beginning of the sixteenth century. The long façade on the canal is dominated by the windows on the first floor (piano nobile), with its fine loggia, which corresponds, inside, to the long side of the salone which faces the outside, a rarity in Venice. The plan is complex: the entrance from the street, with its elegant doorway, and the main water entrance both give onto the portico with its five slender arches opening onto the interior courtyard. Behind this, another building is joined to the main block, forming an L shape, by means of the ingenious solution of two overhead passages, built on top of the surrounding walls; a solution we shall find used later at Ca' Pesaro. The whole building, elegant in its lines and details, is delightfully open and varied from the inside. It reveals an adaptability and a flexibility which are as far from Renaissance canons as they are from other traditional schemes.

47

PAL. CORNER SPINELLI, Mauro Coducci, late XV c. Built at the end of the fifteenth century and the beginning of the sixteenth century and the beginning of the sixteenth by Mauro Coducci, this palace still preserves some traditional characteristics, such as the façade divided into three parts, with the windows in the centre; decoration with shallow later pilasters, marble circles, etc. There are, however some innovations, Tuscan in origin, which were to be used in subsequent buildings, such as the high rusticated base

48

CA' VENDRAMIN CALERGI, Mauro Coducci, 1500-1509. This is one of the most magnificent aristocratic residences on the Grand Canal; it was built by Mauro Coducci at the beginning of the sixteenth century, and completed by Pietro Lombardo in 1509. The side wing overlooking the garden was added later, designed by Vittorio Scamozzi. The main façade, the distribution of windows, and the general effect of lightness, follows many Venetian traditions, both byzantine and Renaissance, while having

of the first two floors, the motif of the double windows contained within an arch, which is repeated on the upper floors. An innovation which was not to be repeated, is that of the delightful trilobate balconies, a horizontal translation of the façade outline so dear to Coducci. The various elements mingled with good taste and a sense of proportion make this palace a jewel of Renaissance architecture on the Grand Canal.

a Tuscan air in the double windows in the arches, the double columns placed between and in the strongly jutting cornice. The entire elaboration of the façade is, however, resolved in an original and coherent manner, so much so as to constitute the starting-point for Venetian architecture of the whole of the sixteenth and seventeenth centuries. Richard Wagner lived and worked in this palace, and died here February 13th 1883.

EARLY XVIth CENTURY ARCHITECTS

There is a period in the history of Venetian architecture which deserves special attention: it goes from the end of the working careers of the early Renaissance architects, such as the Lombardo, Coducci and Rizzo, until the appearance of Sansovino and, later on, of Sammicheli and Palladio; in fact the first three decades of the XVI century. During this period, which is not usually studied in detail, highly talented, if not particularly famous architects, Giovanni Buora, Giangiacomo dei Grigi, Bartolomeo Bon, Antonio Abbondi, known as « Scarpagnino », and Giorgio Spavento, were working in Venice. This generation of architects designed buildings which are sometimes real masterpieces, and nearly always examples of refined taste and of great constructional expertise. Renaissance techniques are applied in a wide variety of buildings: the Dormitory on S. Giorgio, the Scuola di S. Rocco, the Fabbriche Vecchie di Rialto, the Camerlenghi Palace are all, for different reasons, unique in Venetian architecture. The Senators' Wing in the Doge's Palace, the churches of S. Teodoro and S. Fantin are small masterpieces; while the Fondaco dei Tedeschi and the church of S. Salvador are among the highest expressions of XVIth century architecture in Venice, or, indeed, in Italy.

ISLAND OF SAN GIORGIO MAGGIORE

This is the most famous and most beautiful of the Benedictine monasteries of the lagoon. In this island, called Isola dei Cipressi, a small church dedicated to St. George was built at the beginning of the ninth century. In 982 the Doge Tribuno Memmo granted the island to the Benedictine Giovanni Morosini when he came from Spain. In 1109, the relics of St. Stephen were brought here, and each Christmas the Signoria visited the Benedictine Monastery to commemorate this event, with a traditional nocturnal festa. In 1109 the great Doge Sebastian Ziani was buried here. In 1223 an earthquake destroyed all the buildings of S. Giorgio; they were rebuilt by Doge Pietro Ziani, who died and was finally buried here. In the fifteenth century, the rich and powerful monastery of St. Giorgio became a famous study centre; in 1419 the church was restored; in 1433 Cosimo de' Medici, exiled from Florence, was given hospitality here; with him was his architect Michelozzo Michelozzi who built the monastery library, the first Renaissance work in Venice, described by Vasari; this was destroyed by fire in 1614. (See also No. 66 and 96).

49

DORMITORY AND CLOISTER OF THE BAY TREES, Giovanni Buora, 1494-1540. The latter part of the fifteenth century and the first half of the following one saw the beginning of the rebuilding of the whole island of San Giorgio. Only the Cloister of the Bay Trees and the dormitory remain from this first period. The Dormitory or "Manica Lunga" is a two-storeyed building, 128 metres long, which was begun in 1449, was continued by Giovanni Buora in 1494, who realised his masterpiece,

with extraordinary luminous effects in the corridor; the building was finished after Buora's death in 1513. The Cloister, designed by Giovanni Buora himself, was built by his son Andrea from 1516 to 1540; it adjoins the Dormitory, and echoes the spaciousness of the latter with the Foresterie (Guest Rooms) on the South side, the Library to the West side, and the Abbot's apartments to the North with the Chapter House (sala capitolare) below in 1553.

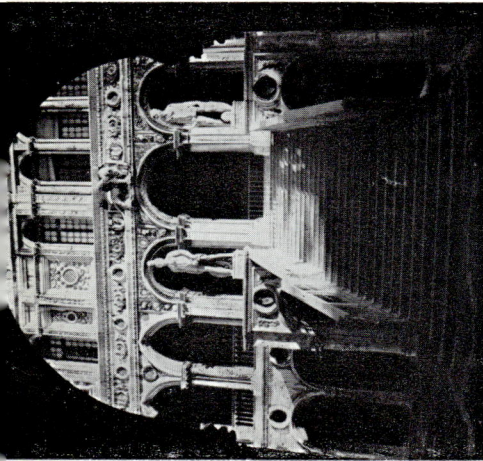

50

THE DOGE'S PALACE, Renaissance Wing 1483-1520. There is almost no interruption in the continuity between the Gothic and the Renaissance parts of the palace; the meeting point of the two styles can be taken as the Foscari Arch, almost symbolically placed between the Porta della Carta and the Giants' Stairway. After the fire of September 14th, 1483, the East Wing was completely rebuilt, in an imposing and ornate style, between the courtyard and the Rio di Palazzo. Antonio Rizzo was the architect until 1498, when Giorgio Spavento and Antonio Abbondi, known as Scarpagnino, succeeded him. Pietro Solari, known as Lombardo assisted in

the decoration, and the wing was finished between 1550 and 1560. Rizzo's beautifully decorated Giants' Stairway, and Spavento's elegant Pregadi Wing which form the delightful courtyard (dei Senatori) both date from the same period. The building stretches along the canal, behind the apses of St. Mark's with the Doges apartments, the sacristy (1486), and Spavento's small church of St. Theodore, a jewel of early sixteenth century architecture. The Scala d'oro (Golden Staircase), designed by Jacopo Sansovino in 1555, and finished by Scarpagnino in 1559, together with the interior decoration of the various halls such as the Hall of the Four Doors,

the Hall of the Collegio and of the Anticollegio rebuilt by Andrea Palladio, and by Antonio Da Ponte after the fires of 1574 and 1577 all belong to a later period. The side of the Foscari Wing, built to replace the open-air staircase which was demolished (1602), the Clock Façade (1603-1614) of Manopola, which continued the portico on the South and West sides of the courtyard, and Antonio Contino's famous Bridge of Sighs, which joins the Doge's Palace to the new prisons, all belong to the beginning of the seventeenth century. (See also No. 23),

62

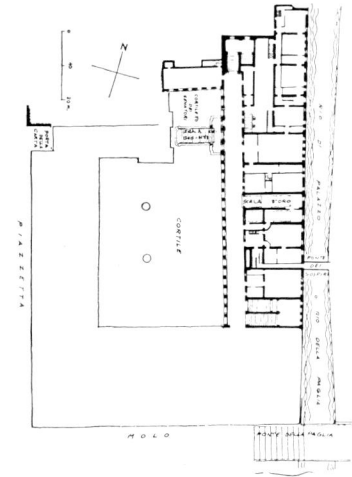

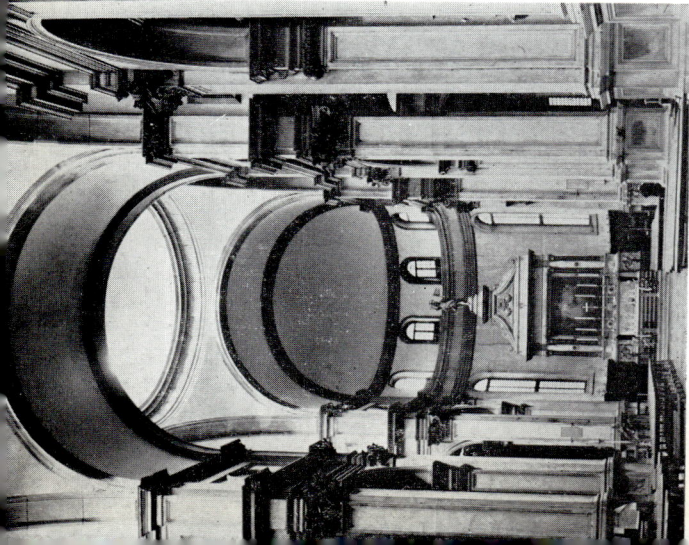

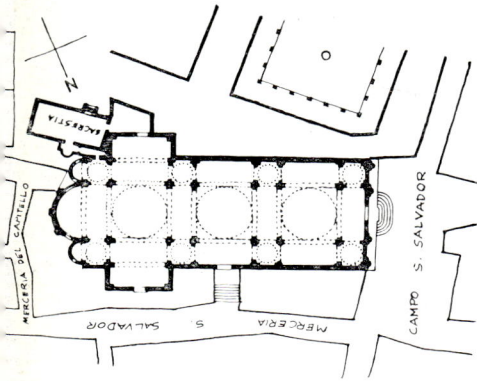

51

SAN SALVADOR, Giorgio Spavento, 1507-1534. This church was founded in the seventh century, rebuilt in the twelfth by the Canons of St. Augustine, and again between 1507 and 1534 in its present form, on a design by Giorgio Spavento, who began by building the presbytery. Later, the work was supervised by Pietro and Tullio Lombardo, and completed by Jacopo Sansovino; in 1574 Vincenzo Scamozzi cut lanterns in the cupolas. The façade was carried out by Giuseppe Sardi in 1663. Spavento also designed the fine, well-lit sacristy. The church itself, one of the most important of the Italian Renaissance, is built over the crypt with a singular plan; a Greek cross, repeated and fused with the basilica plan with three naves. The result is a longitudinal construction, with vaulting and the three alternate cupolas overhead, which opens out at the sides onto three transepts in succession, separated by the groups of four pilasters, which, too, support a small cupola. The pilasters, the cornices and the lintels of the arches, with their clean incisive lines, underline the robust interplay of solids and spaces with magnificent effect. Nearby are the two sixteenth century cloisters, attributed to Sansovino, of the huge convent (now Head Telephone Office), the long façade of which overlooks Rio San Salvador. In the church are to be found famous works of art by Bellini, Tiziano, Sansovino, Vittoria, etc.

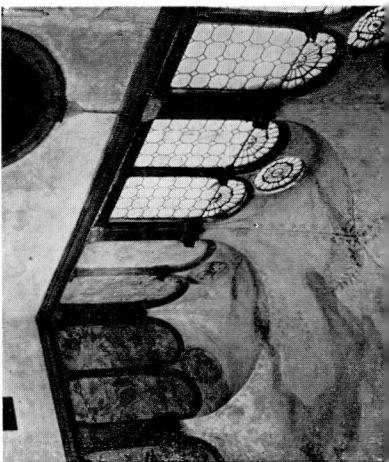

52
SAN FANTIN, Antonio Scarpagnino, 1507-1564. This small church was built with a bequest from Cardinal Zeno; it was begun in 1507 on a design by Antonio Abbondi "Scarpagnino"; after 1549, the apses were continued by Jacopo Sansovino, and finished in 1564. The interesting basilica plan, an extended Greek cross, is rather similar to that of San Salvador, with which it is almost contemporary. Despite its modest proportions, this beautiful church has an imposing, spacious appearance, an extraordinarily well proportioned unit. The building fits admirably into the plan of the small Campo.

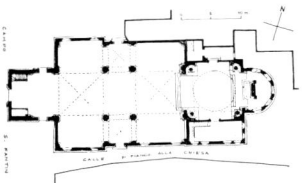

53

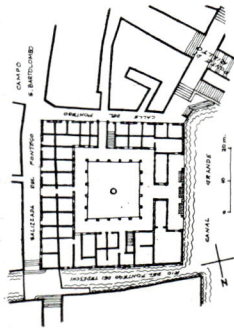

FONDACO DEI TEDESCHI, Spavento, 1505-1508. A typical mercantile building, this was already in existence in the twelfth century; burnt down in 1478, and was rebuilt in 1505-1508, in the first place on designs by Gerolamo Tedesco, soon afterwards substituted by Giorgio Spavento, the Proto (Surveyor) of St. Mark's, whose work was completed by Antonio Scarpagnino. It was carefully restored in 1937, and is now the chief Post Office. The building, a free-standing block, has a square plan, and encloses a courtyard

with loggias. It is an unusual style for Venice. The façades are rather shut-in in appearance, even if they are at the same time elegant in their linear simplicity. Only on the side facing the Grand Canal do the ground-floor portico, the slight side projections, once surmounted by small towers demolished in 1836, together with the crenellation, remind us of traditional Venetian architecture. The façade on the Grand Canal was once decorated by frescoes by Giorgione, and other façades had frescoes by Tiziano which have unfortunately been lost. The feature of greatest interest is the interior **courtyard**, where the uninterrupted series of arches of the portico and the loggias, gradually diminishing in height, lightens the solid mass of the walls, and creates a sense of space which is full of mystery, and at the same time, of classical composure.

54

PAL. DEI CAMERLENGHI, 1525-28. This elegant palazzo was built by Guglielmo dei Grigi of Bergamo between 1525 and 1528, and it was the residence of the three Camerlenghi (magistrates), with the State Prisons on the ground floor. The façades were once inlaid with coloured marble, and the interior was decorated by sixteenth-century paintings. This building, placed in this unique position

adjoining Rialto Bridge, isolated by the bend of the Grand Canal, has all its façades equally elaborately decorated, with identical richness of architectural detail. It is a unique example, in Venice, of a building which has no main façade, sides and back. Its simple proportions are thus emphasised, enhancing the splendour of the decoration.

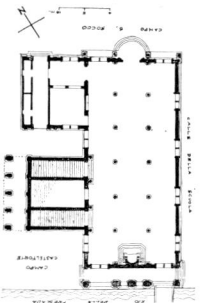

55
SCUOLA DI SAN ROCCO, Bartolomeo Bon and Antonio Scarpagnino, 1515-1560. This is another of the Great Guilds (Scuole Grandi); building was begun in 1515 on the design of Bartolomeo Bon who directed the work until 1524, completing the ground floor level. The work was continued from 1527 until 1549 by Antonio Scarpagnino who built the first floor, the façade and the main stairway. These were completed by Giangiacomo dei Grigi. The façade facing Campo S. Rocco is asymmetrical; to the left, corresponding to the inside halls, the mullioned windows in the style of Coducci on the ground floor, and

the larger ones on the first floor, are set between the strongly jutting fluted columns, and the indentation of the cornice, while the right-hand side has a flatter effect. The back of the building, the work of Scarpagnino, with the addition of the side wings, and the portico on the ground floor makes the building more interesting from a town-planning point of view, and helps to place it with greater naturalness, despite its bulk, in its characteristic Venetian setting. The interior is vast and imposing, especially the stairway, and is transformed by the presence of Tintoretto's masterpieces.

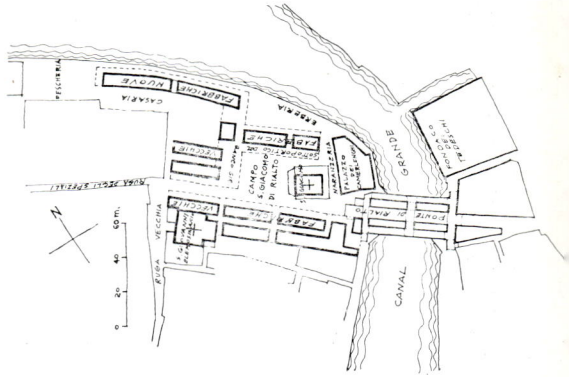

56

FABBRICHE DI RIALTO, Antonio Scarpagnino and Jacopo Sansovino, 1520-1555. The Fabbriche di Rialto consist of the large block of buildings stretching from the foot of Rialto Bridge right round Campo S. Giacomo, and along the Grand Canal. After the fire of 1514, the Fabbriche Vecchie (old) were built from 1520 to 1522, designed by Antonio Scarpagnino. They include the Palazzo dei Dieci Savi (now the Offices of the Water Board) stretching right along the Ruga degli Orefici, and the other similar buildings opposite these, and those surrounding the Campo S. Giacomo, which together form the Portico del Ban-

co Giro. Along the Grand Canal adjoining the Fabbriche Vecchie, are the Fabbriche Nuove, built in 1555 on a design of Jacopo Sansovino. The Fabbriche, with ground-floor porticoes for commercial activity, and the two upper floors for offices of the various public officials concerned with commerce, navigation, and food supplies, form an interesting example of functional architecture. Admirably laid out, they form a well-spaced group of buildings which is, unfortunately, transformed and masked by the temporary buildings of the market which undoubtedly alter the clean Renaissance lines of the original plan

57

SAN GIORGIO DEI GRECI, Sante Lombardo, 1539-1561. The church is part of the interesting group of buildings of the Greek community in Venice; it was begun in 1539 on a design by Sante Lombardo, and completed in 1561: the cupola was added later in 1571. The narrow, high façade is decorated by pilasters, niches and tympani; the sides and the apse have an elegance and purity of line that is still early Renaissance. The interior has a single nave, with the presbytery area marked by the iconostasis, in the Orthodox tradition, and by

the "Barco". In front of, and to one side of the church, stands the churchyard, bordered at the canal edge by a **wall** (c) designed by Longhena in the second half of the seventeenth century. On one side is the bell-tower designed by Simone Sorella (1582-1592), with an adjoining loggia - the only remaining part of the Renaissance cloister. On the other side are two buildings by Longhena: the **Scuoletta Greca** of San Nicolò, and the Flangini Collegio, dating from 1678; the group forms one of the most elegant corners of Venice.

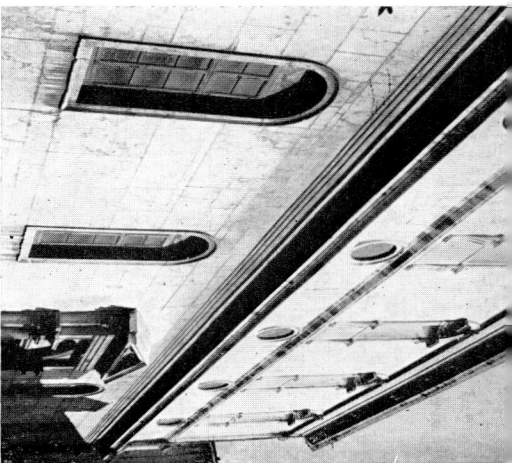

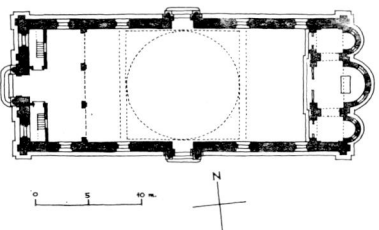

Monument to Rangone by Sansovino at S. Zulian.

JACOPO SANSOVINO

Jacopo Tatti, known as Sansovino (born Florence 1486 - died Venice 1570), sculptor and architect, worked in Florence and Rome, whence he came to Venice in 1527 to become « Proto of S. Marco » (Superintendent of the Works), the highest position an architect could hold. Friend of Tiziano and Aretino, Sansovino had an enormous influence on the world of art and on the new direction architecture was taking in Venice in the second half of the XVIth century. With Sammicheli and Palladio, Sansovino made an important contribution to the pre-Baroque or Mannerist style, with typically Venetian characteristics. Sometimes in the Tuscan manner, as at San Francesco della Vigna, or in the Roman idiom, as in the Library, the Sansovino school of architecture is imbued with plastic and chiaroscuro effects, which lighten the mass of the buildings. It is not fortuitous that Longhena began his Baroque work at Ca' Pesaro using Sansovino's Library and Ca' Corner as starting point.

58
CA' CORNER della Ca' Granda, Sansovino, 1532-1561. This is one of the most magnificent and imposing palaces on the Grand Canal; it was built for Jacopo Cornaro, nephew of the Queen of Cyprus, by Jacopo Sansovino between 1532 and 1561. The solid square mass of the building is situated round an interior courtyard with loggias, in the Tuscan style. The façade on the Grand Canal is divided into three horizontal areas by the entablatures and balconies. The lower part is rusticated and divided into the three vertical

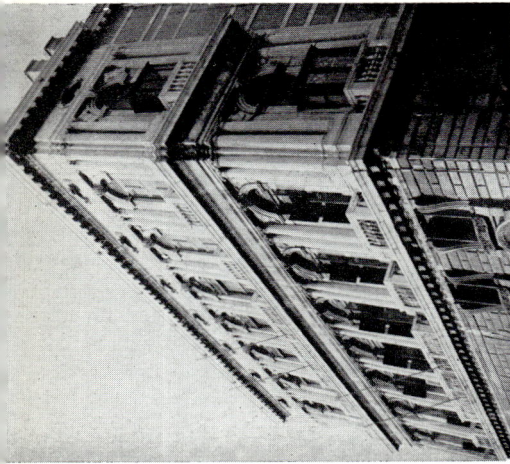

parts traditional to Venetian houses, with the portico in the centre. The two upper floors are marked by the twin columns between the windows, giving an effect of light and shade which lightens the weight of the building. The design of the **south corner** (b), shows Sansovino's sense of urban planning and eye for elegant detail. This architecture can be considered the link between the elegant rhythms of Palazzo Vendramin-Calergi, and the baroque liveliness of Ca' Pesaro.

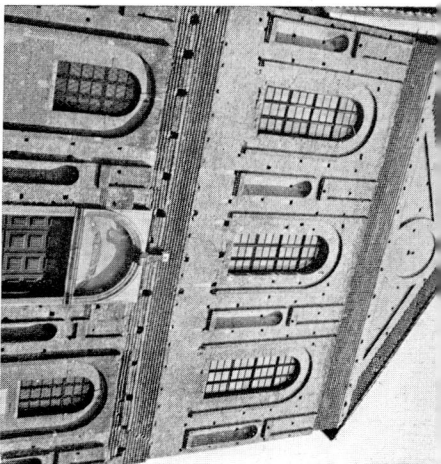

59

MISERICORDIA, Scuola Nuova, Jacopo Sansovino, 1523-1583. Also known as the Scuola di Santa Maria in Val Verde, this was one of the six 'Scuole Grandi' (Great Guilds). It was begun in 1532 on a design of Jacopo Sansovino, and the interior was completed in 1583, when it was inaugurated by Doge Nicola Da Ponte. The exterior was never finished. At present, the ground floor of the building is used as a warehouse, and the upper floor as a gymnasium. Even though unfinished, the exterior has an air of massive dignity: the high brick wall is marked by jutting parts and recesses forming abstract patterns. Inside, the ground floor is divided into naves by high columns without losing anything of its imposing spaciousness; the effect is completed by the great stairway.

a

60

S. FRANCESCO DELLA VIGNA, Sansovino, 1583, Palladio, 1568-72. The original church was built in 1253, on the spot where, according to tradition, a small church commemorated the arrival of the evangelist St. Mark from Aquileia. The present church was begun in 1534 on a design by Jacopo Sansovino; the imposing façade was carried out between 1568 and 1572 from a design by Andrea Palladio. It is the only example in Venice, apart from the Redentore, of a façade built to Palladio's original design. It rises from the base in smooth squares, and with central tympanum and sloping sides, reflects accurately the interior divisions of space. This

b

was to become the model for many other church façades right up to the eighteenth century. The plan of the church, which shows Tuscan influences, is of a latin cross with a single nave, bordered by five chapels on each side. The presbytery and choir, set well back, probably follow the plan of the original church. On the left side of the altar, the Giustiniani chapel of 1478 contains important Lombardesque sculpture. The interior of the church, in its geometrical purity, achieves perfectly balanced proportions, and has extraordinary strength and spaciousness. It is one of the few buildings the plans of which have been preserved, designed in accordance with the canons of geometrical perfection of Renaissance philosophy (Wittkower 1962). On the north side are the convent cloisters with their simple medieval lines. The campo, to the south, is particularly interesting, surrounded by buildings of various epochs: besides the church with its campanile (1581), there is the Gritti family palace (1525), once the residence of the Apostolic Nuncios; the Oratory of the Holy Stigmata of the seventeenth century, and the overhead gallery supported on columns, Palladian in style, built in the early nineteenth century.

72.

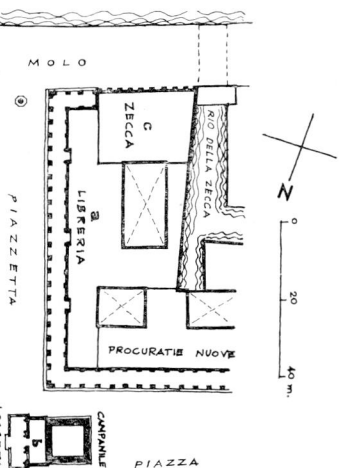

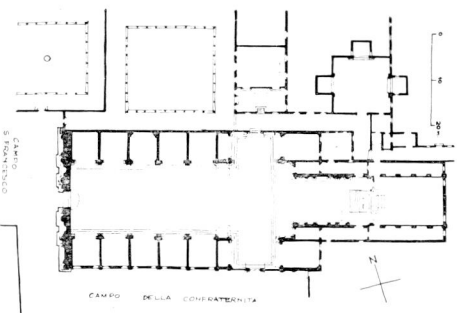

61
LIBRARY, ZECCA, LOGGETTA, Piazza San Marco, Sansovino, 1537-1588.

The **Library** (a) is one of the finest of Sansovino's works in Venice; it is a long low building with twenty-one arches, Doric arcade on the ground floor, and Ionic columns on the first floor, with balustrade and statues above. Its proportions are similar to those of the old Veneto-Byzantine buildings which once surrounded the Piazza, but here the interpretation is completely new, with rich, substantial forms, almost baroque. It was begun in 1537 to house the precious codices bequeathed by Cardinal Bes-

sarione; the building was interrupted in 1545 when a vault fell in; this was later substituted by a flat-beamed ceiling. By 1554, the building had reached the sixteenth arch from the campanile, and was taken up again by Scamozzi, who completed the part facing the lagoon between 1583 and 1588. From the State entrance under the eleventh arch, its doorway decorated by two caryatids, we climb the sumptuous stairway to the rooms on the upper floor to the Vestibule, with decorated ceiling, (1550-1560), which has in the centre Titian's « Wisdom ». It was turned into a museum in 1597 by Vincenzo Scamozzi. The

b

c

Gilded Hall, with walls decorated by portraits of philosophers by Jacopo Tintoretto, the ceiling decorated by the works of seven different painters including Paolo Veronese, now houses an important collection of early miniatures and incunabula, including the famous Grimani Breviary.

The **Zecca** (c), Mint, had been in existence at St. Mark's since 1277; the present building was designed by Jacopo Sansovino, originally on two floors, with rusticated arcading on the ground floor, and half-columns of the Doric order on the upper storey; later another storey with Ionic columns was added by

Sansovino himself. The National Marciana Library has been housed here since 1905; one enters through the doorway at the seventeenth arch, designed by Vincenzo Scamozzi, with two huge 'telamoni' on either side. The architecture of the Zecca is sturdy and severe in character, almost a military building, both the façade overlooking the lagoon, and that facing the interior courtyard (the present-day reading room) where once stood the fine well-head which is now to be found at Ca' Pesaro.

The **Loggetta** (b), was built at the base of the campanile in the fifteenth century as a 'Ridot-

to dei Nobili' (meeting-place for the nobility), in the place of the wooden stalls and shacks; between 1537 and 1549 it was rebuilt by Jacopo Sansovino, and in 1569 it became the guardhouse of the Arsenalotti during the sittings of the Maggior Consiglio. It was transformed in 1663 by the addition of the terrace and balustrade, (the bronze gates date from 1735-7). This small but elegant building, decorated by allegorical statues and the group of the Virgin (bronze by Sansovino himself) was destroyed in 1902 when the Campanile collapsed; it was rebuilt in 1912, using the original material.

74

MICHELE SAMMICHELI

Michele Sammicheli (Verona 1484-1559), civil and military architect, is one of the most important figures in Venetian architecture. Sammicheli was working in Rome from 1500 to 1519, then in Verona from 1520, where he designed the Canossa, Pompei and Bevilacqua Palaces as well as the Porta Palio, and was in Venice from 1535 onwards. Besides the Fort of S. Andrea, he built fortifications at Corfù and Candia for the Republic. Due to his experience in Rome with Sangallo, and his studies of ancient monuments, as well as his work as a military architect, Sammicheli has a robust style and a functional simplicity which often achieves monumental effects. In Venice, from the severe architecture of Palazzo Corner at S. Polo, he went on to build the more elegant Palazzo Gussoni Grimani della Vida on the Grand Canal, culminating with the splendid Palazzo Grimani. Here the monumental proportions are tempered, one might even say made Venetian by the vibrant counterpoint of the subtle modelling of the decorative elements with the dramatic play of solids and voids. It was Sammicheli, perhaps because he came from the Veneto, who best succeeded in adapting the canons of classical architecture to Venice.

62
FORT OF SANT'ANDREA, Sammicheli, 1543.
The fort of Sant'Andrea, also known as Castel Nuovo is part of the defence system of the fortifications of the Serenissima, for the port of San Nicolò on the Lido. Opposite the tower: in fact, there stood the Castel Vecchio; between them was a line of chains blocking the entrance, supported by a pontoon armed with cannons, the so-called "Gaglian-drà". The fort of Sant'Andrea is the work of Michele Sammichele, and was built in 1543;

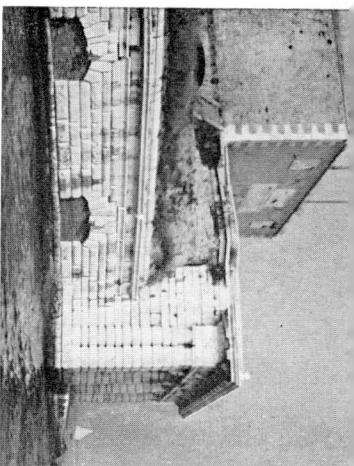

some additions were made after the Battle of Lepanto (1571). The fort consists of an arched bastion, with apertures at water-level for the cannons; in the centre is the main tower: in front of this is a kind of rusticated pronaos, divided into two parts by Tuscan half-columns, with sturdy triglyph entablature: this gives an air of dignity to a strictly military building. While being entirely functional, this building has an imposing unity in its spacious lay-out.

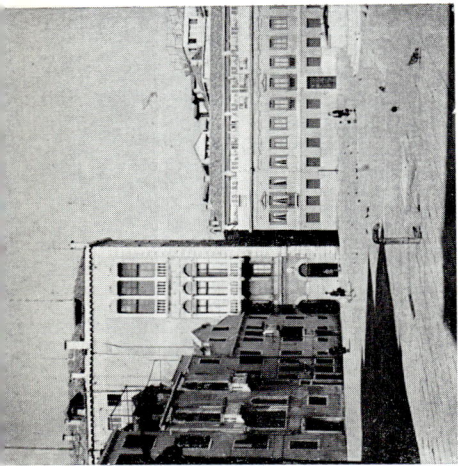

63

PAL. CORNER MOCENIGO, San Polo, Sammicheli, 1559. This palace was built for Giovanni Corner, nephew of the Queen of Cyprus, by Michele Sammicheli in 1559, on the site of an earlier house, once inhabited by the famous general Gattamelata, and later by the duke of Sforza. This robust building, now the premises of the National Customs offices, stretches from the Rio San Polo to the Campo of the same name, forming a C shape, following a traditional Venetian plan. The main façade overlooks the canal; it is quite different in character from traditional Venetian architecture: the ground floor is rusticated, like a fortification; the floors above are designed in a more open way; ionic pilasters, short architraves, inset balustrades, and storey divisions give a close, angular effect round the two central Venetian windows resulting in a sturdy, well-planned building.

64

PALAZZO GRIMANI, Grand Canal, Sammicheli, c. 1550. An enormous building designed by Michele Sammicheli, generally considered to be his masterpiece in Venice; begun half-way through the sixteenth century, the second floor was completed by Giangiacomo dei Grigi after the death of Sammicheli in 1559: the whole was practically finished in 1561. The palace has a rectangular plan, built on a narrow site between the Grand Canal and the Rio of San Luca, on a traditional plan, divided into three by the central rooms, but made asymmetrical by the side courtyard.

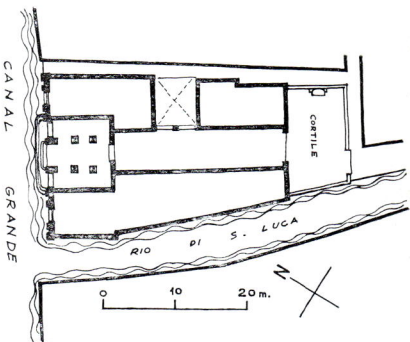

The three exposed façades are all designed with stately grandeur, including the one over-looking the entrance courtyard, an unusual feature in Venice. The main façade on the Grand Canal is divided into three storeys, by the strongly jutting cornices, supported by grooved Corinthian pilasters on the ground floor, and by ionic columns on the upper floors. The simplification of the windows is astonishing: a tripartite Venetian window on each floor, with only two windows at the sides: thus a grandiose effect is achieved, together with a rare sense of unity.

ANDREA PALLADIO

Andrea Palladio (Padua 1508 - Vicenza 1580), architect and scholar, is the outstanding figure in XVIth century Venetian architecture. His works and his principles were destined to have a great influence on the architecture of later centuries, both inside and outside Italy. Palladio's training took place in Vicenza and in Rome, where between 1541 and 1547, he made a study of ancient monuments. Palladio worked first of all in Vicenza (Basilica, Palazzo Chiericati); from 1561 onwards he was in Venice (Carità Convent, S. Giorgio, S. Francesco della Vigna, Redentore). Later he worked again in Vicenza (Valmarana and Thiene Palaces, Loggia del Capitanio, Olympic Theatre) and all over the Venetian region (Villa La Rotonda, Villa Barbaro at Maser, Villa Piovene at Lonedo, Villa Emo at Fanzolo, Villa Malcontenta near Venice, etc.). The enormous and varied production of Palladio as an architect was accompanied by his work as a scholar, collected in the « Four Books of Architecture » published in 1570, which had as much influence as his actual buildings. Palladio's art is based on rigorous classical principles, though these were interpreted bearing in mind the different functional requirements of each building, hence the great variety of his designs. The splendid architecture of the Venetian villas and of the churches in Venice provides some of the happiest and most original achievement in the history of European art.

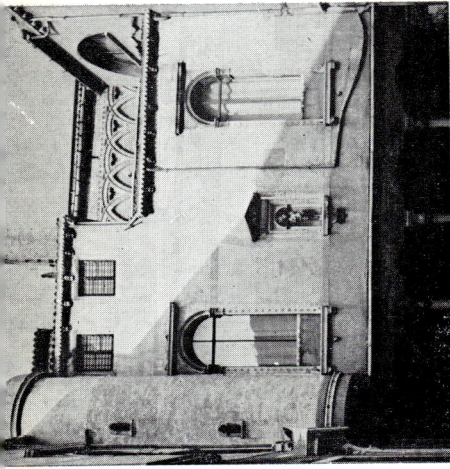

65
CONVENTO DELLA CARITÀ, Palladio, 1552.
The ex-convent of the Carità has been part of the group of buildings of the Accademia since 1807; together with the **church** (a) and the Scuola. The Accademia was founded in 1750, and from 1756 until 1807 was housed in the ex Fonteghetto della Farina at St. Mark's. The convent buildings were transformed in 1552 by a magnificent design of Andrea Palladio. The conversion was never finished, indeed the courtyard with peristyle which Palladio had built to one side of the church was destroyed by fire. Further alterations were made by Selva in 1808-11 and again a few decades ago. Of Palladio's first work in Venice there remains the wing between the spacious courtyard and the rio terrà, the interior spiral staircase, and the tablino; one only survives of the two which were to have been built. The succession of wide archways of the portico and loggia, which open onto the **courtyard** (e) one above the other, follows in the tradition of ancient Roman architecture. The extraordinary use of solid brickwork in

c

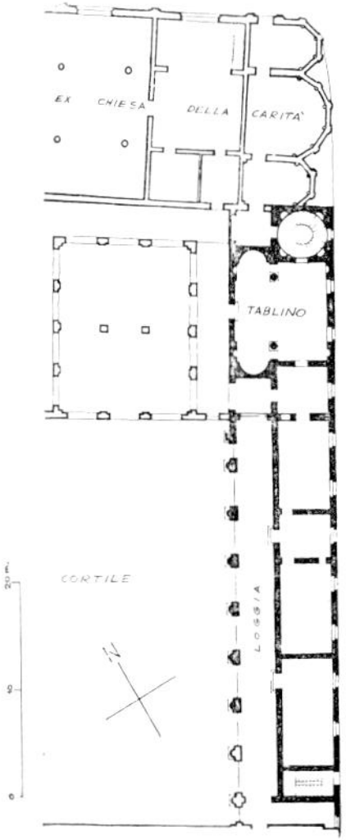

the upper storey, with small windows placed above the arches, are in a way, an interpretation, in Renaissance forms, and with more imposing dimensions, of the Venetian building tradition. The small **tablino** (d) consists of two different areas, joined together by means of the solid curving of the walls and cornices. The **staircase** (c) is built on an oval plan, and is a masterpiece of constructional eloquence and harmonious spatial development in its simplicity.

d

e

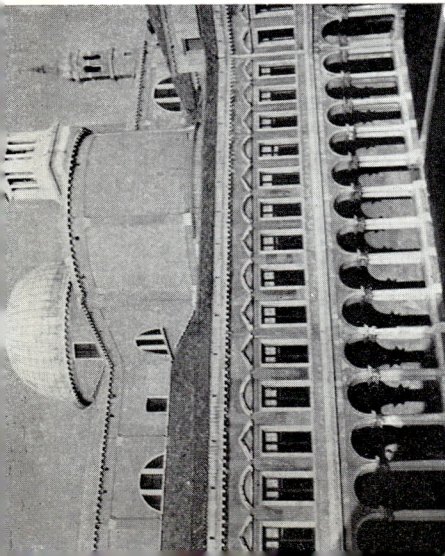
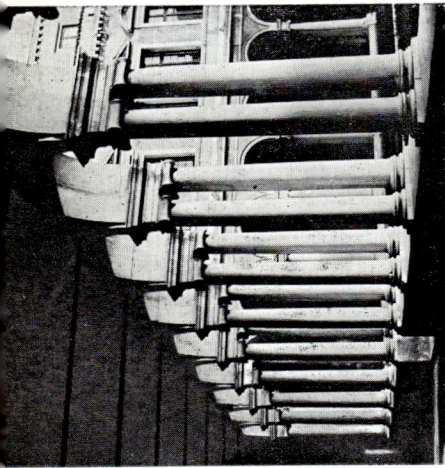

a

66

S. GIORGIO MAGGIORE: Refectory, Cypress Cloister, Church, Andrea Palladio, 1559-1614. Library and staircase, Longhena, 1641-1653.
The second period of restoration of the island of San Giorgio took place during the last half of the sixteenth century, and the beginning of the seventeenth, with the work of Palladio and Longhena. Palladio's first work at San Giorgio was the large Refectory (1559-1563), an imposing hall, gradually introduced by the portico, the stairway and the entrance hall; here Veronese's painting of the « Marriage of Cana » was hung. The **Cloister of the Cypresses** (a/b) is also by Andrea Palladio, begun in 1579 and finished in 1614 after Palladio's death in 1580; it includes the 'Foresterie Nuove' the New Guest Rooms, looking

out onto the lagoon, which were intended as ceremonial rooms for political purposes, it resembles thus the courtyard of a sumptuous palace, rather than a religious cloister. In 1566 Palladio began building the new church, the **façade** (d) of which was completed by Simeone Sorella in 1610, who did not entirely follow the original design. The Palladian church faced a different direction from the fifteenth century one, having its façade towards St. Mark's, it assumes a new scenic role from a town-planning point of view. The church has three **naves** (f), transept and central dome; beyond the presbytery and the row of columns, lies the spacious, elegant **choir** (e). The church is very long, with the floor levels progressively raised so as to

achieve a constant variation of depth, light and space between the nave, transept presbytery and choir. The resulting architecture is at once imposing and theatrical, carried out with extraordinary clarity.
In 1641 Longhena built the **Grand Staircase** (c) to the west side of Palladio's cloisters; with one imposing sweep, most unusual in Venice, it gathers in a single spatial unit the cloister portico and the loggia above. From 1641-53 Longhena rebuilt the Library in the wing which joins the two cloisters; it was enriched in 1665-71 by the shelving designed by the German carver Francesco Pauc. (See also No. 49 and 96).

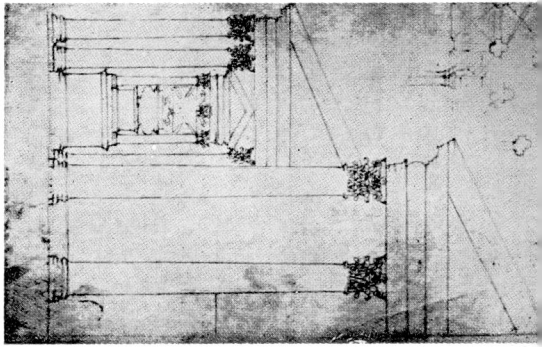

d Palladio, Design for the façade of S. Giorgio Maggiore, Royal Institute of British Architects, London (From R. Wittkower, « Architectural Principles »).

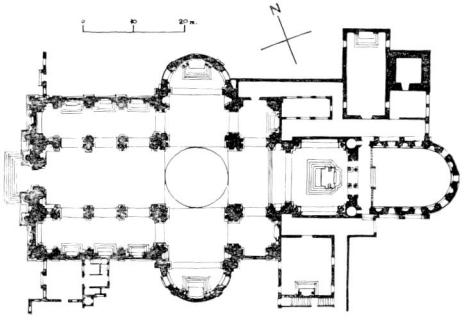

e

67

CHURCH DEL REDENTOR, Giudecca, Palladio, 1577-1592. The Senate ordered the building of the church of the Redentore after the plague in 1576; together with that of the Salute, it is a classic example of a votive temple. Redentore was visited annually by the Signoria on the third Sunday in July, thus giving rise to the famous Festa del Redentore, a night gala on the Giudecca canal. The building was begun in 1577 on a design by Antonio da Ponte, carried out in collaboration with Palladio, and it was consecrated in 1592. The imposing façade rests on a rusticated pediment, with a wide flight of steps, like a Venetian country house; its architectural lines are severely simple in the clear contrast between rectangular and triangular geometrical lines. In the other parts of the building such as the sides, the buttresses, the transept, the apse, the dome and the small bell-towers, the geometrical simplicity is strongly accentuated. The interior, a mixture of a longitudinal and central plan, consists of a single nave, flanked by three chapels on each side, the presbytery with exedra transept, the great dome overhead, and the choir situated behind the Corinthian colonnade of the central exedra. The nave, presbytery and choir are all on different levels, but are united in a single spatial conception. The church is considered to be the masterpiece of the religious architecture of Andrea Palladio.

CANALE DELLA GIUDECCA

FONDAMENTA DELLE ZITELLE

N

68

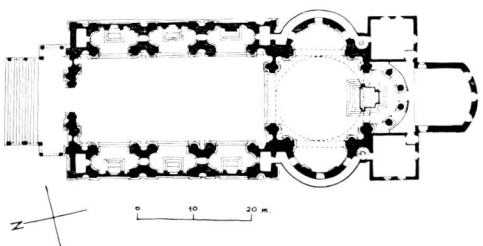

CHURCH OF THE ZITELLE. A. Palladio, 1582-86. The church is part of the hostel of the Zitelle (spinsters), a benevolent home for the education of poor Venetian girls. The project is by Palladio, the building was directed by Jacopo Bozzetto from 1582 to 1586. The church is built on a square plan with corners rounded for acoustic reasons, because concerts of religious music were held there as at the Pietà (90) and similar institutions. It is covered by a single large dome with two small side bell-towers. The church and the hostel are an architectural unit, the church in fact is surrounded on three sides by the hostel which forms a delightful courtyard with porticoes behind the apse. The façade of the church with its side buildings on the Giudecca Canal is simple and harmonious, following the interior space and harmonious, following the interior space divisions. The dimensions of the bell-towers on the façade, framed by the hostel, are thus justified, they would otherwise be out of proportion.

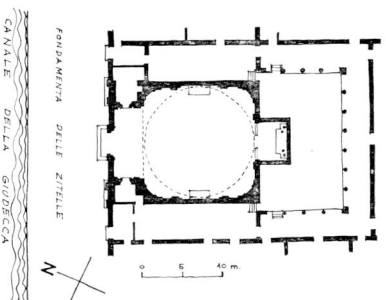

69

SAN PIETRO DI CASTELLO, Smeraldi and Graspigia, 1596-1619. A church dedicated to Sts. Sergio and Bacco already existed on this island, called by the ancient name of 'Olivolo', dating from the seventh century. Rebuilt several times, it was the see of the Bishop of Venice, 'Olivolense', who, in 1451, received the title of Patriarch of Venice, which derived from that of Grado. This church was therefore, the cathedral of the city up to 1801 when the bishop's see was transferred to St. Mark's. The present-day church was begun in 1596 when Francesco Smeraldi began work on the façade which reminds

us of Redentore; the plan, with three naves, transept and dome, recalls rather that of San Giorgio. Taken as a whole, however, it is a work of remarkable stylistic integrity and solemnity. Adjoining the church is the Patriarchal Palace, with the simple sixteenth century cloister, which has been a barracks since 1807, and is now completely abandoned. Isolated in the square stands the elegant leaning tower, rebuilt by Coducci between 1482 and 1488; it once had a terminal cupola which was demolished in 1670; it remains one of the finest and best proportioned bell-towers in the city.

70

RIALTO BRIDGE, Antonio Da Ponte, 1588-1591. Rialto Bridge was for many centuries the only permanent link between the two banks of the Grand Canal; originally in the twelfth century there existed a bridge on barges; halfway through the century this was substituted by a wooden bridge, with a central drawbridge (this can be seen in the famous painting by Carpaccio). Many times reconstructed and repaired, the last time by Giorgio Spavento in 1501. In 1524 it was decided to rebuild it in stone. Michelangelo, Palladio, Vignola, Sansovino, Da Ponte, Scamozzi and others submitted designs; it fell to Da Ponte to build the bridge with the help of his nephew Antonio Contino. The work was car-

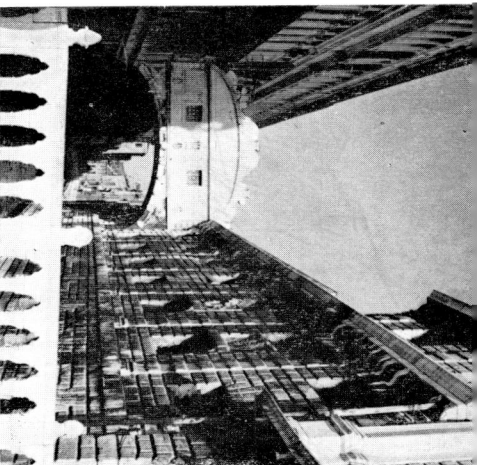

ried out between 1588 and 1591. The bridge, with a single-arch span of 28 metres, supports two rows of shops under twelve small arches in each row, with two large arches joining the arcades in the centre. Thus there are three streets for pedestrians; one between the two rows of shops, and two facing outwards with views down the Grand Canal, the total width of all three is 24 metres. From an architectural point of view, the bridge is both heavy and imposing; but its value goes beyond its intrinsic merits of form: by now it is an integral part of the Venetian townscape; indeed, it might be considered symbolic, uniting as it does water and pedestrian transport.

71
THE PRISONS and the Bridge of Sighs, Da Ponte and Contino, 1563-1614. The Prisons were built at the end of the sixteenth century to enlarge the state prisons already in the city, and the part overlooking the Riva degli Schiavoni as offices for one of the oldest types of magistrate "I Signori di notte al Criminal", whose duty was to safeguard citizens, especially during the night. The building was, therefore, a necessary expansion of the Doge's Palace, to which it was directly joined by the famous Bridge of Sighs. Work was begun on the interior in 1563 by Giovanni Antonio Rusconi; it was continued by Antonio Da Ponte in 1589, and completed by his nephews Antonio and Tommaso Contino in 1614. The façade overlooking the rio is rusticated with pilasters of a sturdy simplicity; the main façade on the Riva sorts oddly with the rest of the building behind. It consists of a portico with rooms above, and from the outside has a solid calm appearance, its large well-spaced windows continue the rhythm of the older buildings in St. Mark's Square. The Bridge of Sighs is the work of Antonio Contino, carried out at the turn of the century. The new, supple baroque forms are used here with naturalness, adapted to a construction hanging in mid-air above the water.

72

PALAZZO BALBI, Vittoria, 1582-1590. This splendid palazzo, was built "in volta de canal" (on the bend of the Canal) - one of the finest positions on the Grand Canal. It was built for Nicolò Balbi from 1582 to 1590 by Alessandro Vittoria, more famous as a sculptor than as an architect. The ground plan and the design of the façade follow traditional lines, divided into three, but with a new style feeling towards plastic forms, and liberated from classical outlines. This can be seen in the details: the multiple pilasters and square panels between the windows: the projecting interrupted tympani of the windows and side doors: the cartouches and volutes surrounding the windows and above the central doorway, with the arch reaching up to the tympanum, the two family coats of arms at the sides, and the oval windows beneath the cornice. These details come partly from the school of Sansovino, and were to be further developed during the baroque period by Longhena.

73

PAL. CONTARINI DEGLI SCRIGNI, Canal Grande, Scamozzi, 1609. There are two Contarini degli Scrigni palaces on the Grand Canal, right next to each other; that on the right is late Gothic dating from the second half of the fifteenth century, the interior restored by Smeraldi in the early seventeenth century. That on the left was built in 1609 by Scamozzi, and is the more interesting of the two, even if it is disparaged by purists for classical proportions. It has, in fact, been

74
P..OCURATIE NUOVE, Scamozzi, 1586-1616, Longhena 1640. The Procuratie Nuove occupy the south side of St. Mark's Square; they were divided in nine apartments, arranged round interior courtyards for the nine Procuratori of St. Mark's. Designed by Vincenzo Scamozzi on the site of the old Ospizio Orseolo, a building in the Veneto-byzantine style, demolished in 1582, the Procuratie were begun in 1586 with the construction of the first ten arches near the campanile. When Scamozzi died in 1616, the building was continued by Baldassare Longhena in 1640, who completed it right to the end of the square, including the seven arches adjoining the church of St. Geminiano, demolished in 1810. The architecture of the Procuratie Nuo-

ve takes up the motif of Sansovino's Library, raising it by one floor, but achieving a quite different effect, more similar to the Convent della Carità, but here with a more imposing and decorative effect, in the real baroque manner. It is significant that the part carried out later by Longhena, without the decoration on the top storey, is almost more Palladian in manner than that of Scamozzi. It is interesting to observe how the same type of architecture was used in Venice with few variations during the course of three centuries, even if with differing results: the Library in the sixteenth century, the Procuratie from the sixteenth to the seventeenth century, and the Napoleonic Wing at the beginning of the nineteenth century (See No. 61 and 95).

adapted, in its storey-levels, to the neighbouring Gothic building. Having only a limited frontage, the lines of the façade have a vertical character, accentuated by the smooth twin pilasters. However, this verticalism is present too in the small interior façade, and in the volumes of the building as a whole, culminating in the small tower of the oval staircase. Here we have integrity of design and taste, well ahead of its time, besides heralding the baroque style, it is already strangely in harmony with the neoclassical style of the eighteenth century.

BALDASSARE LONGHENA AND THE BAROQUE

The architect Baldassare Longhena (Venice 1598-1682) is the leading figure of Venetian Baroque. He succeeded in developing coherently the lessons learnt from the work of Sansovino, Scamozzi and, especially, Palladio, in a way which particularly suited the Venetian setting. The basis of his work is clearly classical, though this does not exclude a lively wealth of sculptural decoration. Palladian elements are used by Longhena not only in the design of his façades, but, also, in the complex interplay of spatial elements of his interiors, as in the church of the Salute or in the Staircase at S. Giorgio. The prolific genius of Longhena was given free rein in the buildings for various religious and foreign communities resident in Venice, such as the Scuola dei Carmini, the Greek School, the Somaschi Convent at the Salute, the Domenican Convent at SS. Giovanni e Paolo, the Synagogues in the Ghetto. The work of Longhena was continued by Antonio Gaspari (Ca' Pesaro) and Giorgio Massari (Ca' Rezzonico), but also found followers in Giuseppe Sardi gnon and Andrea Cominelli were the second and Domenico Rossi, while Alessandro Tremignon and Andrea Cominelli were the second generation of the Baroque style which developed in Venice between the XVIIth and the XVIIIth centuries.

75

CHURCH OF THE SALUTE, Baldassare Longhena, 1631-81. This church, dedicated to the Blessed Virgin of the Salute, was built by decree of the Senate of 1630 as a thanksgiving for delivery from the danger of the plague. Eleven designs were submitted: that of Baldassare Longhena was chosen. The church, built on the site of the Ospizio della Trinità, was begun in 1631 and finished in 1681. In the same year, the square in front of the church, and the embankment on the Grand Canal were laid out and completed. The Basilica was consecrated on November 9th 1687 (Longhena had died in 1682). The Signoria made a solemn visit every year to the church, crossing the Grand Canal on a bridge of barges; the occasion became a popular festival, and is still observed by Venetians.

The church has a centralised plan: it is thought that Longhena took his inspiration from a woodcut by Polifilo (1499). Round the central octagonal space, covered by an enormous dome, is the ambulatory, from which the six radial chapels open out; the high altar is theatrically placed in a raised, isolated position, between the exedra, cover-

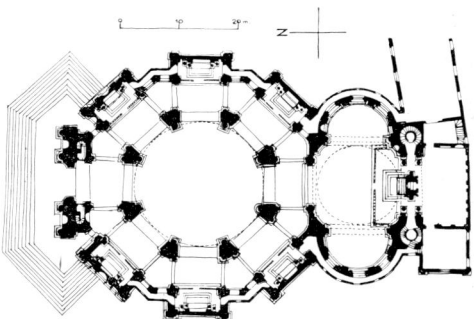

ed by a dome, and the rectangular choir area. The exterior is majestic and imposing, raised on a pediment with a flight of sixteen steps leading up to the main doorway. The radial chapels each have a tympanum and window: above is the octagonal drum surrounded by sixteen volutes which serve as buttresses and are highly decorative. There are also two cupolas with lanterns, and two small side towers; all these have become unmistakable parts of the Venice skyline. The numerous statues and ornamental figures are like the pinnacles of a Gothic cathedral, strictly linked to the architectural conception of the whole.

The church of the Salute, with all its originality, is the fruit of a culture which is rooted in the far-off paintings of Perugino and Raffaello, in the drawings of Jacopo Bellini, or in the works of Carpaccio and Gentile Bellini. Many Palladian elements, too, are recognisable: the main prospect with the intersection of the orders, side chapels with windows, the small bell-towers, the design of the apses. As with all important works of art, this one, too, marks the end of a period of taste in Venice - that of Mannerism, and opens the new Baroque period which was to have such fruitful development.

76

CA' PESARO, Longhena-Gaspari, 1676-1710.
Designed by Baldassare Longhena for the powerful Pesaro family, this palace is the masterpiece of baroque civic architecture in Venice. The building of it lasted over fifty years; it was begun in 1676 from the wing in the courtyard (Giovanni Pesaro had been Doge since 1652) but it was interrupted in 1682 by the death of Longhena and of his client Leonardo Pesaro, at the point when the first two storeys of the façade on the Grand Canal had been built. The work was taken up again in 1709 under the direction of Antonio Gaspari, who in 1710 completed the third storey of the façade, and built the parts overlooking the side canal, and at the

far end of the courtyard, with some variations from Longhena's design (for example the stairway was moved to one side instead of being in the centre of the hall). The palace passed to the Gradenigo family and then to that of La Masa and was finally left as a bequest to the city in 1889, it now houses the International Gallery of Modern Art, and the Museum of Oriental Art. The building forms a « C » shape round a courtyard, being bounded by the Grand Canal, the Rio delle Due Torri, and the Rio della Pergola incorporating several older buildings. The wing on the Grand Canal follows the traditional division in three parts, with a central hall, but the façade is a single mass with two "piani no-

bili", a vigorous style full of "chiaroscuro" effects, above the rusticated ground floor. The wing overlooking the Rio delle due Torreselle, follows the slight curve of the canal, thus acquiring, despite its mass and the break with the main façade, an integrity of its own. The courtyard is particularly striking, with its Sansovino well-head taken from the Zecca. Around it are the walls with the hanging gallery, portico and the loggias of the upstairs halls, and the balconies of the different floors. These various elements, merge together to form a splendid enclosed palace courtyard.

77
CA' REZZONICO, Longhena-Massari, 1667-1785.

This palace is, together with Ca' Pesaro, one of the baroque masterpieces on the Grand Canal. It was begun in 1667 on a design of Baldassare Longhena for the Priuli-Bon family, and the building work went on for almost a century. In 1682, on the death of Longhena, it had reached the first floor level; in 1750 the palace was bought by the Rezzonico family, and work was begun again under the direction of Giorgio Massari, after having been interrupted for several decades. This architect, after having completed the second floor of the façade, designed the side overlooking the canal and the Great Stairway.

In 1758, to celebrate the occasion of Carlo Rezzonico's election to the papacy as Clement XIIIth, the palace was finally completed. In the 19th century, the building passed through the hands of various owners, amongst whom was the English poet Robert Browning, who died here in 1889. In 1935 it was acquired by the Municipality of Venice, to house founded the Eighteenth Century Venetian Museum here. The main façade has three storeys, separated by projecting cornices; the ground floor is rusticated, and the upper floors are given variety by columns, arcades and balconies, creating an effect which is sumptuous and picturesque at the same time.

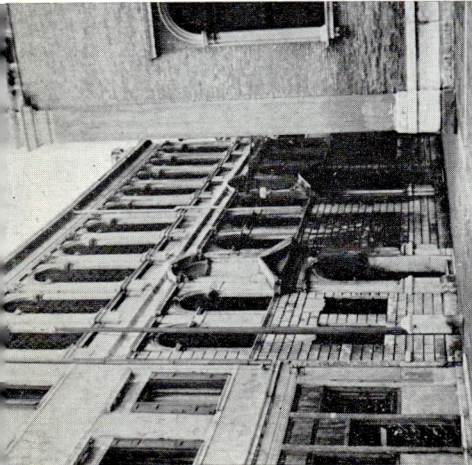

78
SCUOLA DEI CARMINI, Cantello-Longhena, 1627-1670. The Confraternity of Santa Maria del Carmelo, which dated from 1597, commissioned Cantello to design the Scuola in 1627. The work was interrupted by the plague in 1629, but in 1638 the building was inaugurated, even though it was still unfinished. The interior was finally completed in 1663. Between 1668 and 1670 the façades were built, designed by Baldassare Longhena. In 1739 the decoration of the great hall ceiling was entrusted to Giambattista Tiepolo: he completed the famous series of paintings in 1744. In 1767 the Scuola was numbered amongst the Scuole Grandi (Great Guilds). The rectangular building is divided on each floor into two parts; on the ground floor

there is the Hall on the right, while to the left is the Staircase, Sacristy and smaller rooms. On the first floor there is the assembly room with the altar on the right, while on the left is the Hall of the Hostel, and the Archive Room. The most interesting part of the interior is the beautiful divided staircase, open at the sides, its barrel-vaulted ceiling with stucco decoration by Stazio. From the outside the two façades are completely different one from the other; the part looking onto the church is plain and functional, the other towards the Rio Terra is sumptuous and imposing. The latter façade is reminiscent of the other Scuola built by Longhena, the Scuola dei Greci.

79
SANTA MARIA OF NAZARETH (SCALZI), Longhena-Sardi, 1600-1680. Designed by Baldassare Longhena for the Carmelite Scalzi friars, the church was dedicated to Santa Maria of Nazareth because of an image brought from the island of Lazzaretto. The building, begun in 1660, was directed by Longhena until 1673, the façade, designed by Giuseppe Sardi, was carried out between 1672 and 1680: inside, the high altar was completed by Fra Giuseppe Pozzo and the ceiling decorated with frescoes by Giambattista Tiepolo (1743), destroyed in 1915. The church was consecrated in 1705; it has a single nave plan with six side chapels. The façade with two orders of twin columns, with niches and statues between them, resembles that of Santa Maria in Campitelli in Rome, by Rinaldi (1656).

80
THE SYNAGOGUES of the Ghetto. 16th century - 17th century. The Ghetto, obligatory dwelling place for Jews, was founded in 1527 on the site where a foundry for cannons stood, called "getto" or "ghetto"; a name which was afterwards used throughout Europe. Divided into old and new quarters, the houses of the ghetto were inhabited by five thousand people; they are buildings of extraordinary height and density, and together form a most interesting piece of town planning. In the Ghetto, moreover, are to be found the Synagogues, or "Schole", which, divided into various rites and nationalities, form the oldest,

richest and most numerous group of synagogues existing in the world. The **Schola grande Tedesca** (c) 1528; the "Schola Canton" of 1532, the "Italiana" of 1575, the **Levantina** (b) of 1538, transformed in 1635 by the elegant exterior decoration probably by Longhena, and furnished by Brustolon; the **Spagnola** (d) or Ponentina of 1555 which was remodernised by Longhena in 1654. The latter boasts, besides the usual rich interior decoration, oriental in taste, an oval matroneo like the contemporary theatres in Venice and in Emilia at that period.

81

CHURCH OF GESUITI, Rossi, 1715-28. On the site where a 12th century church of the Order of the Crociferi had stood, the present church dedicated to Santa Maria Assunta was built between 1715 and 1728 for the Jesuit order which had acquired the nearby convent. The design is by Domenico Rossi, assisted by Fra Pozzo, Dorigny, and Torretti. The façade, built with money given by the Manin family, was planned by Giambattista Fattoretto. The church, built by the Jesuits themselves, shows the characteristics of the church of this Order throughout the world, derived from St. Ignazio in Rome: a single nave, flanked by side chapels, transept and presbytery united in a spacious central area, magnificent decoration with stuccoes and frescoes on the vaulted and domed ceiling, rich altars placed in the niches (the central one inspired by Bernini). The façade, too, with its sturdy columns, strongly projecting cornices, and numerous statues of angels and saints above, forms a typical example of inter-national baroque, unusual for Venice.

82

CHURCH OF THE TOLENTINI, Scamozzi 1591, Tirali 1706-14. This church, dedicated to St. Nicholas of Tolentino, and the convent of the Teatine fathers, who had come from Thiene with St. Gaetano in 1528, were built by Vincenzo Scamozzi between 1591 and 1602. The convent, recently restored, is now the home of the University Institute of Architecture. The interior of the church, Palladian in inspiration, is on a Latin cross plan, with the crossing of nave and transept covered by a dome, demolished in the 17th century. The rich stucco decoration, and most of the paintings, date from the 17th century; the altar is the work of Longhena. The façade of the church was added a century later in 1706-14, from a design by Andrea Tirali. It uses, for the first time in Venice, the pronaos with six grooved Corinthian columns, and overhead tympanum, which, Roman in origin, had been recently used by Palladio (e.g. Villa Malcontenta at Fusina). This architectural element was to become extremely popular with English architects few years later (e.g. St. Martin-in-the-Fields, London, 1722-26).

83
CHURCH OF ST. GEREMIA, Corbellini, 1753-1809. In the place of an earlier 13th century church (in existence), the present church was begun in 1753 on a plan of Abbot Carlo Corbellini of Brescia. The building went on for a long time: in 1759 the building was half finished; in 1760 the first mass was celebrated; in 1768 work began again and continued until 1807; the two façades were finished in 1871. The church has

a Greek cross plan: the four arms, covered by domes, finish in an exedra; in the centre is the oval dome, with four small domes at the sides. From the outside, the building has a vigorous series of volumes and curves which reflect the articulation of the interior. It is one of the last expressions of baroque in Venice. The church of S. Geremia, with Palazzo Flangini and Palazzo Labia at its sides, forms one of the most interesting groups of buildings on the Grand Canal.

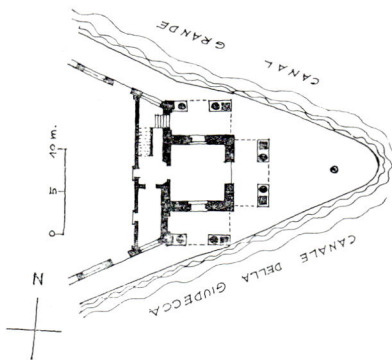

84

PUNTA DELLA DOGANA, Benoni, 1677. The "Dogana da Mar" was rebuilt in 1677 by Giuseppe Benoni, better known as a hydraulic engineer, and winner of the competition in which Longhena, Cominelli and Sardi had taken part. The Customs building, with the tower on the point towards the lagoon, was already in existence (as can be seen from the map of de Barbari), and was formerly part of the defence system of the city; chains were placed from this point to the opposite side of the canal in order to block the Grand Canal. The building is still used as a customs house; the only example of a civic building which has maintained its original function over the centuries. This small building which, from a town planning point of view, is the apex of the triangle of the Salute island has the sturdy appearance of a military construction: the tower nucleus, however, has been masked and lightened by the porticoes which open out on all three sides. The crenellated sides, the volutes and on the top the globe supported by figures help to break up the silhouette of the building. Defensive elements such as crenellation or reminders of the sea, like the globe, here become purely decorative townscape forms.

85

PAL. SURIAN-BELLOTTO, Rio di Cannaregio, Sardi, late 17th century. Built towards the end of the 17th century probably by Giuseppe Sardi, this palace is one of the most splendid along the wide canal of Cannaregio, which is certainly the most beautiful in Venice after the Grand Canal itself. The palace boasted, like others in this area, a large garden; in the 18th century it was the residence of the French ambassador, and Jean Jacques Rousseau lived here. The façade is extraordinarily protracted; divided into three parts, in the traditional manner, with Venetian windows in the slightly projecting storey; it has an additional wing on the right, thus obtaining a pleasing asymmetrical effect. Taken as a whole, the rectangular lines, the floor divisions, the balconies and the shallow rustication give the building a calm, orderly appearance, which harmonises with its setting.

a

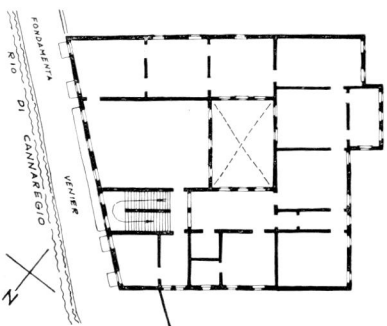
b

86

PALAZZO PRIULI-MANFRIN, Rio di Canna-regio, Tirali, 1735. Palazzo Priuli-Manfrin, situated at the Ponte delle Guglie, was rebuilt at the beginning of the 18th century, and is a late work of the architect Andrea Tirali (died in 1737). It has some unusual features; the plan of the rooms does not follow the usual division into 3 parts, but surrounds an interior courtyard, functionally logical (the staircase, for example, is placed at the front of the building). The façade, with its rectangular lines and the flat, undecorated squares, seems to be a forerunner of modern architecture. Cut out rectangles on smooth wall surface were not new to Venice; even without

going back to Palladio's façade for the Redentore we only need recall some of Longhena's façades, or the top floor of nearby **Palazzo Savorgnan** (c) by Giuseppe Sardi a few decades before; but this is the only example in which the entire façade is designed in this rigorous way. If it were not for the presence of the balconies and the cornice, it would be difficult to date this work, whose value goes beyond its intrinsic merits. It does, in fact, give us a glimpse of resemblances, as yet not sufficiently studied, with the most advanced European architecture of the 18th century.

c

87

PALAZZO PISANI, S. Stefano, Manopola 1614, Frigimelica 1728. The palace is one of the most rich and sumptuous of the city, even if it is not on the Grand Canal. It was begun in 1614-15 on a design of Bortolo of Venice, called "Manopola". In 1728 the upper storeys facing the campo were added, as well as the extension towards the Grand Canal, with interior courtyards and loggias under the direction of Girolamo Frigimelica, who at that time was building the famous villa at Stra on the Brenta for the same family. In 1793, the interior was remodernised by Maccaruzzi. The palace is now the Music Conservatory « Bendetto Marcello ». Despite the fact that it was built in different periods by different personalities, the main façade has an architectural unity of its own and the interior has well planned halls, courtyards, stairs, ballroom etc. The most interesting features are the airy loggias, one above the other, which, with the two courtyards, form a single spatial conception.

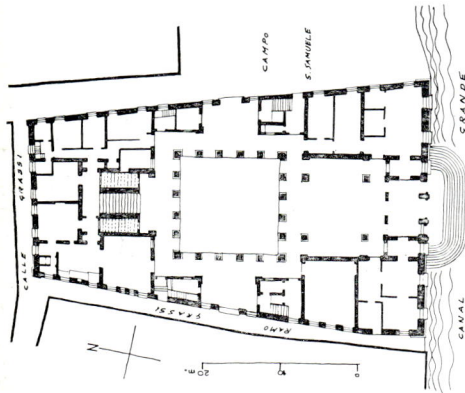

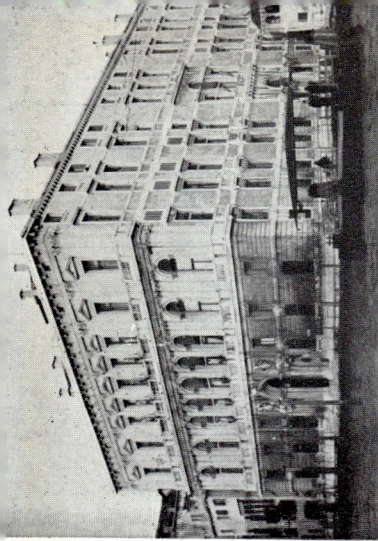

THE 18th CENTURY AND GIORGIO MASSARI

The XVIIIth century was a most fertile period for Venice in the field of art, a second Golden Century comparable to the XVIth century itself; and this contrast to the disastrous political situation which brought about the fall of the Republic in 1797. In the world of painting the names of Tiepolo, Canaletto, Guardi, Piranesi stand out; in music we have such prominent composers as Benedetto Marcello and Antonio Vivaldi; in the theatre Carlo Goldoni and Carlo Gozzi; in art criticism Carlo Lodoli and Francesco Algarotti. In architecture, there were many, often contrasting figures working in Venice during the XVIIIth century. There were those continuing the Baroque style like Carlo Corbellini or Bernardo Macaruzzi, or Neo-Palladian like Lorenzo Boschetti. There were other architects who were turning away from Palladianism towards neo-classical purism, like Andrea Tirali, Giovanni Scalfarotto, Antonio Visentini and Tommaso Temanza. It is against this background that the figure of Giorgio Massari (Venice 1686-1766) stands out not only for his prodigious activity, but also because he epitomises all the aforementioned tendencies, working now in the Palladian style, like the Villa Lattes at Istrana, or La Cordellina at Vicenza, now theatrically grandiose like the Gesuati Church or Palazzo Grassi, and now elegant like the Pietà church. Massari's art can be taken as the symbol of an incomparable civilisation which in the XVIIIth century ended gloriously, using up all its last splendid opportunities of expression.

88

PALAZZO GRASSI, S. Samuele, Massari 1748-1772. Built by Giorgio Massari for the Bologna family of Grassi, this palace is the most splendid example of an aristocratic 18th century residence, just before the fall of the Venetian Republic; it represents the swansong of Venetian secular architecture. The building, begun in 1748, was enlarged in 1766 and completed in 1772 after the death of Massari (1766). It is now a Centre for Arts and Costume. The building is trapeze shaped, round the beautiful internal courtyard, with a plan which differs from the traditional Vene-

tian one, perhaps going back to Sansovino's design for Ca' Corner. The façade, with its rigid studied lines is not as interesting as the interior areas, especially the ground floor. From the steps going down to the Grand Canal, one crosses the portico and the pronaos to reach the interior courtyard with its colonnades; opposite is the divided staircase leading to the first floor, with its loggia overlooking the courtyard. The ground floor plan of Ca' Rezzonico is here improved on and rendered more harmonious.

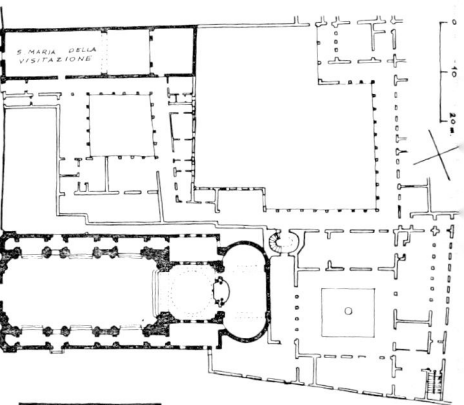

89
GESUATI CHURCH, Zattere, Massari, 1726-1736.

This church, dedicated to Santa Maria del Rosario, was built from 1726 to 1736 on a design of Giorgio Massari for the Dominican Friars, who in 1668 had taken the place of the "poor Gesuati" here since 1392. 18th century religious art finds its highest and most coherent expression in this church. The facade and apses are Palladian in style; while the interior, with the beautiful altar strategically placed between the well-lit nave and the choir exedra takes its inspiration from Longhena's Salute, and from Gaspari's Santa Maria della Fava. The elegant interior decoration, of the same period and in the same

S. MARIA DELLA VISITAZIONE
FONDAMENTA DELLE ZATTERE

style as the architecture, is completed by the series of altarpieces painted by Tiepolo, Piazzetta and Ricci, and the sculpture of Morlaiter, together with Tiepolo's frescoes on the vaulted ceiling. They form an entire group of masterpieces still in the original position for which they were designed. Adjoining the church are the interesting cloisters of the convent, now a Craft school; from them the small church della Visitation can be reached (1493-1524): an elegant example of Renaissance architecture, in the manner of Coducci; the decorated ceiling is a rare example of the Umbrian school of painting in Venice.

100

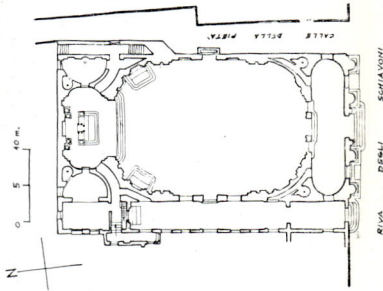

90

CHURCH DELLA PIETÀ, Riva Schiavoni, Massari, 1744-60. The new church della Pietà and the adjoining Foundling Hospital, were designed in 1735 by Giorgio Massari. The church was built between 1744 and 1760 on the site of an earlier 15th century church. The Hospital, a charitable institution where orphan girls were given a musical education, was left unfinished. Famous concerts were held in the Pietà church, as they were in Palladio's church delle Zitelle, and in Scamozzi's St. Lazzaro dei Mendicanti. Antonio Vivaldi (1675-1743) was one of the conductors of these concerts, and chorus-master and violin teacher in the Hospital. Thus these churches attached to Hospitals were also

concert halls, and this accounts for their structure: rounded angles to the walls, low vaulted ceilings, and entrance hall to isolate the concert hall from the outside, and choir stalls for the singers and musicians. All these characteristics are present in the church della Pietà where Massari, taking his inspiration from Sansovino's Ospizio degli Incurabili (demolished in the 19th century) and from Gaspari's church della Fava, has created a masterpiece of 18th-century architecture; Massari, designed all the details of the interior decoration as well. The elegance of the architecture is enhanced by Giambattista Tiepolo's famous frescoes on the ceiling (1754-1755).

NEO-CLASSICISM AND THE XIXth CENTURY

Neo-classical tendencies soon show themselves in Venice; some symptons can be noticed in the early decades of the XVIIIth century, e. g. Palazzo Manfrin by Tirali, or the church of S. Simeon Piccolo by Scalfarotto. In the second half of the century interesting works, like the Maddalena church by Temanza, were built. This early tendencies of Venetian architecture towards neo-classical forms can be explained by the Palladian tradition, which had its home in Venice and was always making its presence felt to a greater or lesser degree. The frequent cultural contacts with England may also help to explain this tendency. The key figure in the continual exchange of works and artists is the British Consul Joseph Smith, for whom Visentini built a palace on the Grand Canal. At the end of the XVIIIth century and the beginning of the XIXth, neo-classical architecture in Venice is led by Gian Antonio Selva and by his numerous pupils and successors. The political and economic situation, caused by the fall of the Republic and by the French and, later, Austrian occupation, did not allow the high quality of early XIX century architecture to be fully expressed. In the second half of the XIXth century, academic eclecticism took over also in Venice. An occasional point of interest is provided by Neo-Gothic which heralds the Art Nouveau style and hence the future development of modern architecture.

91
ST. SIMEON AND ST. JUDE (Piccolo), Scalfarotto, 1718-1738. Built on a design by Giovanni Scalfarotto between 1718 and 1738 this church is one of the earliest examples of neo-classical architecture in Venice. The circular plan with pronaos was originally inspired by the Pantheon in Rome; the presbytery area, with exedra transept, small dome

and bell towers, is inspired by the Salute church. The pronaos with a high pediment and flight of steps is Palladian in style, similar to the church of Tolentini (82). As a whole, however, this church is new in style, especially as regards the clean rigorous lines of the architecture, which betrays the influence of the growing spirit of the Age of Reason.

92
CHURCH DELLA MADDALENA, Temanza, 1760. This small church is one of the few works of Tommaso Temanza, better known as an historian than as an architect; it was built in 1760 on the site of an earlier 13th century church. Temanza, who died in 1789, was buried here. This church too, has a circular plan; it is inspired by the Pantheon, like the church of S. Simeon Piccolo; in fact here the influence of the Roman temple can be

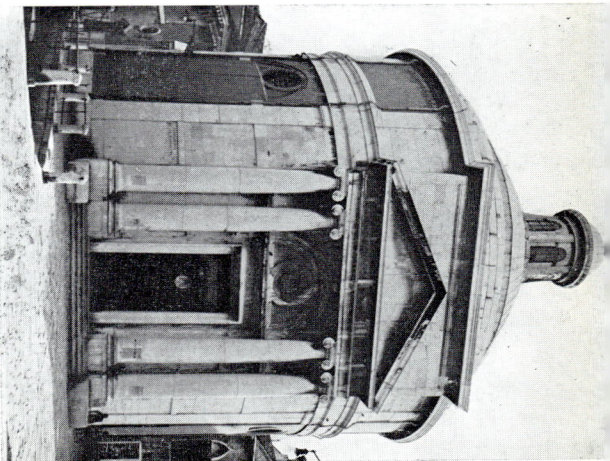

more strongly felt. The mass of the building is more compact and geometrical than the other church, because of the reduced pronaos flattened against the façade. The purity of line and form is even more striking than that of S. Simeon, as one would expect from a theoretician. In the interior, the minute proportions, like those of an oratory, are enlivened by chapels placed round the hexagonal perimeter, and by the oval presbytery.

93
CHURCH OF S. MAURIZIO, Zaguri, Diedo, Selva, 1806-1828. This church had already been rebuilt in 1590, on the site of an earlier building; in 1806 it was again demolished and rebuilt, changing the orientation of the façade which had previously faced the canal; it was consecrated in 1828. Based on designs of the patrician Pietro Zaguri, taken from Sansovino's church of S. Geminiano which had recently been demolished in Piazza San Marco. The project was modified by Antonio Diedo and Giannantonio Selva. It has a Greek cross plan, contained within a square perimeter, with a small semicircular apse; the four arms are vaulted, while the centre, with the four angles, are covered by a dome; the plan is similar to that of Coducci's San Giovanni Grisostomo. The façade is more original, in a pure neo-classical style.

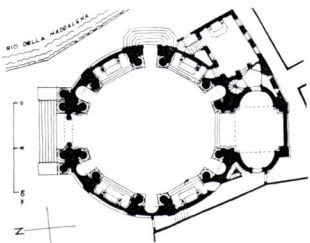

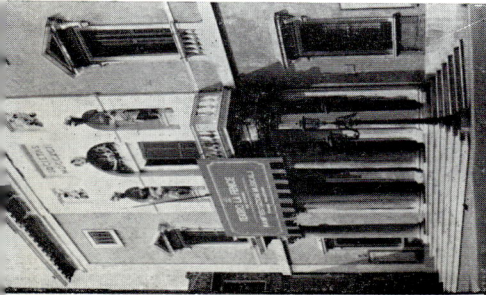

94

THE FENICE THEATRE, Selva, 1790-92. The theatre, one of the most famous in Europe, was built on a design by Giannantonio Selva between 1790 and 1792; in 1836 it was destroyed by fire, and was faithfully rebuilt by the brothers Tommaso and Giambattista Meduna, pupils of Selva; in 1937 the interior decoration and the stage equipment was improved by Nino Barbantini. The theatre extends from Campo S. Fantin to the Canal della Verona, and is planned round the large oval auditorium with a seating capacity for 1500. There is, too, the pronaos, an entrance hall, smaller rooms, the largest of which is the beautiful Sala Apollinea, and the great staircase. The façade facing the square, with the small pronaos and columns, and that overlooking the canal with an arcaded portico, are designed with good taste. In its interior, on the other hand, the theatre shows a freer, more original, use of space, unprejudiced by traditional considerations of symmetry and balance, while still adhering to the neoclassical style. This is an extraordinary example of functionalism before its time. It must have been incomprehensible to the closed architectural circles of that period.

95

NAPOLEONIC WING, Piazza San Marco, Antolini, Soli, Santi, 1810-11. The Napoleonic wing occupies the short side of the Piazza opposite that of the Church; here once stood Sansovino's church of S. Geminiano, which had on its right the continuation of the Procuratie Vecchie, and to its left the last five arches of the Procuratie Nuove. These buildings were demolished in 1807 on Napoleon's orders, in order to build a ballroom for the Royal Palace which was situated in the Procuratie Nuove. The Napoleonic wing was begun by Giovanni Antolini from Milan, and was continued after 1810 by Giuseppe Maria Soli from Emilia. After the Restoration (1815) the work was completed by Lorenzo Santi of Siena. The façade facing the Piazza repeats the arch motif of the Procuratie

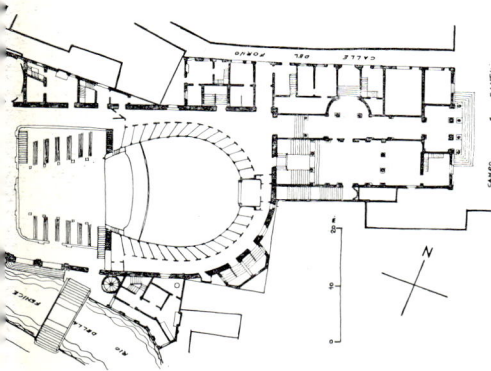

Nuove, substituting an attic floor decorated by reliefs for the third storey. The façade facing the Bocca di Piazza has, on the other hand, lines which are clearly classical, in the Palladian tradition. The porticoes on the ground floor complete the spaces of the Procuratie Nuove and the Piazza as a whole in a pleasing manner, while the Procuratie Vecchie are completely separate in style. From the porticoes one climbs the imposing staircase to reach a square ante-room, and thence the Ballroom itself. This splendid formal hall, with its oval balcony goes back to 17th and 18th century models, such as the Villa Pisani at Stra, it forms a typically refined example of the fashion throughout the Courts of Europe at the beginning of the 19th century.

96

SAN GIORGIO: Bell tower, Buratti, 1791; Harbour, Mezzani, 1810-15. The third phase in the rebuilding of the island of S. Giorgio (the first was in 15th and 16th centuries, the second in the 16th and 17th centuries) in the neoclassical style began in 1791 with the bell tower designed by Benedetto Buratti from Bologna. The elegant lines of the belfry and the even simpler geometrical lines of the steeple (cylinder and cone) began that anticipated modern architecture which international fashion in architecture anticipated modern architecture by more than a century. The Benedictine convent was suppressed in 1806 after having been the site of the Conclave in which Pope Pius VII was elected; in 1810 the island was made a Free Port. With this aim in view the harbour was constructed, with the two towers and the buildings nearby by Giuseppe Mezzani, a

pupil of Selva. The low, carefully constructed buildings facing the lagoon melt into the background and the older ones which they adjoin. The harbour, on the other hand, being a functional construction is an architectural novelty, an open space defined with linear purity at the water's edge. It completes the architectural unity of the island, and incorporates it into the area of the St. Mark's pool. Other neo-classical buildings overlook the basin, the small café building on the shore of the Royal Gardens, built by Lorenzo Santi about 1830, the new customs warehouses and the Salt storehouse on the Zattere (i Saloni) reconstructed by Giovan Alvise Pigazzi in 1855. These are well-designed buildings; the quick rhythm of their arcades re-echoes their interior space divisions (see also No. 49 and 66).

a

97

THE XIX CENTURY BRIDGE-HEAD. The building of the railway bridge in the middle of the XIX century enabled Venice to be directly connected to the mainland by land for the first time. This link has brought a great change to Venice, by moving the main point of arrival, which had up to then been S. Marco, facing South, to the Northern part towards the mainland. In this part of the city a kind of bridge-head has been formed giving rise to a transformation which is still in course. Houses were pulled down and canals filled in, to make room for the new buildings. Among the buildings which were demolished, not always with good reasons, was Palladio's church of S. Lucia on the Grand Canal. Of the new constructions, besides the railway bridge, we illustrate two functional structures contemporary with it: the slaughterhouse and the warehouses at the end of the Grand Canal. The old railway station and the bridge over the Grand Canal, interesting examples of iron architecture, have since been demolished.

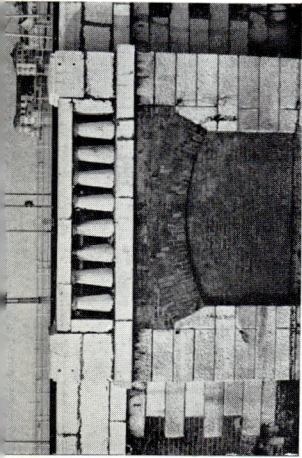

a) Railway Bridge, T. Meduna, 1841-46. The Railway Bridge, designed by Tommaso Meduna and Luigi Duodo, was built between 1841 and 1846 by Antonio Petrich as the terminal of the Milan-Venice railway line. This line was not finished however until 1857. The bridge stretches for 3.5 km over the lagoon between the area of S. Giobbe-S. Lucia and S. Giuliano on the mainland, near another interesting XIX c. construction, the Fort of Marghera. Completely straight, it is built on a series of Istrian stone arches. The stone cutting, especially on the arches and the balustrades, is in the Neo-Classical style. This bridge, with its functional and constructional merits, is one of the few good examples of XIX century architecture in Venice.

106

b) Warehouses on the Grand Canal. These warehouses, still in use, were erected between 1850 and 1880 when the Marine Terminal of S. Basilio was built, between the Giudecca Canal and the Railway Station of S. Lucia. These warehouses, which are utilitarian in character, still belong, together with the Slaughter-House, to the functional tradition of the Neo-Classical period.

c) The Slaughter-House, G. Salvadori, 1842. The Slaughter-House was built in 1842 by Giuseppe Salvadori, head of the Architectural Department, and designer of the Malibran Theatre. It is formed by several small one-storey buildings joined together. The façades, carefully designed, are in pure Neo-Classical style, but the symmetrical, rational plan of the Slaughter-House is surprisingly modern.

98
BUILDING IN SALIZZADA S. MOISÈ, mid XIXth c. This commercial building is an interesting example of the Neo-Gothic style. Gothic influence is to be found here in the outline of the arched lintels, in the small low arches with the edged mouldings, in the light structuralism of the building as a whole. Neoclassical influence can be detected in the arches, in the cornices and in the modillions. But the prevalence of windows and the regular design of the façade, however much they betray the Veneto-Byzantine influence, clearly have a modern stamp, which strangely resembles some buildings of the Chicago School. The decoration in cast iron, on the arches and balconies, and in the interior staircase, have a pleasant "art nouveau" air. The most Venetian characteristic of the building is the way it is adapted to the urban scene; in fact it incorporates a small archway quite unselfconsciously, which helps to render the series of arches on the ground floor delightfully asymmetrical.

99

THE BIENNALE PAVILIONS. The gardens of the Biennale, the International Art Exhibition first held in 1895, are the site of several pavilions built in various periods by the exhibiting countries. A number of these are of remarkable architectural interest, by important architects such as Hoffmann, Rietveld and Aalto. Thus we have an interesting and varied group of buildings designed for an identical purpose. It should be noticed that the Biennale pavilions are an isolated group of buildings which have no connection with the urban scene of Venice. In Louis Kahn's project for the Conference building and the new Italian pavilion, recently presented in Venice, for the first time the architecture of the Biennale is conceived as part of the city with its canals and lagoon. The pavilions of Austria, Finland, Holland and Venezuela are here illustrated as, perhaps, the most significant from an architectural point of view. To these the following can be added, all built since the war: Israel, by Richter (1952), Switzerland, by B. Giacometti (1952), Japan, by Y. Takamasa (1956), Canada, by Belgioso, Peressuti, Rogers (1958), Scandinavian Countries, by S. Fehn (1962), Brasil, by N. Marchesini (1964).

Works by Carlo Scarpa, 1948-68. Carlo Scarpa's collaboration with the Biennale from 1948 onwards has been almost continuous, both in the setting out of one-man shows (that of Klee in 1948 was memorable) and in the alterations made from time to time in the Italian pavilion and elsewhere. Of these alterations the Ticket Office and gates, the interior courtyard (1952) and the recent Central Hall (1958) still remain. In the garden Scarpa has designed two isolated buildings, the Art Book Pavilion and the Venezuela Pavilion. The **Art Book Pavilion** (1950) in his inventive capacity shows Scarpa's admiration for Wright. The **Venezuela Pavilion** (1954) is one of the finest and most original of Scarpa's Works, it was unfortunately tampered with in 1968 and Scarpa's harmonious spatial sequence round the portico and the two halls of different heights are now hardly recognisable.

Austria, J. Hoffmann, 1934. This pavilion built in 1934 is one of the last works by Joseph Hoffmann, the master of the Viennese Secession (1870-1956): in its unobtrusiveness can be seen the elegance typical of Hoffmann. It exemplifies three very different, almost contradictory aspects: that of the Secession in the typically corrugated surfaces, contrasting with the glazed opening above; the classical aspect in the symmetrical plan, the square doorway and the elegant arches of the entrance hall; the rationalist aspect can be seen in its clear plan, the spatial purity of the interiors and in the rectangular form facing the canal.

Holland, G. Rietveld, 1954. This pavilion was built by Gerrit Thomas Rietveld, the architect of « De Stijl » movement, in 1954. This building lacks the formal neo-plastic freedom of his famous Utrecht villa, but it is designed on rigorous geometrical relationships, based on the cube: 16x16 m in plan, 16x8 the façades, etc. The geometrical rigour is redeemed by the "turbine" plan, with the side parts on varying levels which gives a dynamic quality to the structure. The central area, lower than the rest, allows indirect lighting which, for an exhibition pavilion, is very functional.

Finland, A. Aalto, 1956. Pavilion designed by Alvar Aalto, prefabricated in Finland and assembled in Venice in 1956. A timber structure easily dismantled because it was intended for one exhibition only. The building is in the form of a trapeze, the walls of vertical panels are sustained by three triangular struts with apex downwards. The roof and the lighting are ingenious: a double screened skylight gives light to the side walls leaving the central area of the pavilion in the half-light. Although designed as a temporary structure in its building technique and details (e.g. door handles) it exemplifies first class architecture.

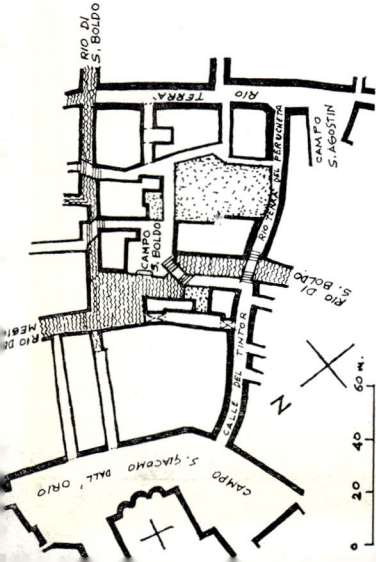

VENETIAN TOWNSCAPE

While describing individual buildings in Venice, the urban environment has already often been mentioned. In fact every building in Venice is not fully comprehensible if it is not seen in the urban scene of which it forms a part. There are however in Venice innumerable examples of townscapes which are particularly successful from a spatial and figurative point of view without having any building of great architectural interest. One example is given here of these urban masterpieces, that of Campo S. Boldo, where the various constructional and spatial elements are intermingled in an extremely natural way.

100

CAMPO AND RIO S. BOLDO. This is a typical corner of Venice where the possibilities of water and land transport exist side by side, as generally happens in all the squares of Venice still served by canals. The urban function of this clearing transport centre is evident, it serves commercial areas like Campo S. Giacomo dall'Orio, Calle del Tintor, Rio Terrà della Parrucchetta and the S. Agostin area. There are similarly functional centres in Venice, but in this case the widening of the square and the canal pool are of roughly the same size, as are the water

and land outlets leading off them. This similarity of size allows the two areas to be side by side without one being more important than the other and to form a single urban area. The bridge, the most important element in S. Boldo, bends gracefully to facilitate the water and land traffic. The townscape is here especially enriched by small gardens with trees behind their surrounding walls. The human dimension of the buildings too contributes to the fascination of this corner of Venice although it has no architectural masterpiece.

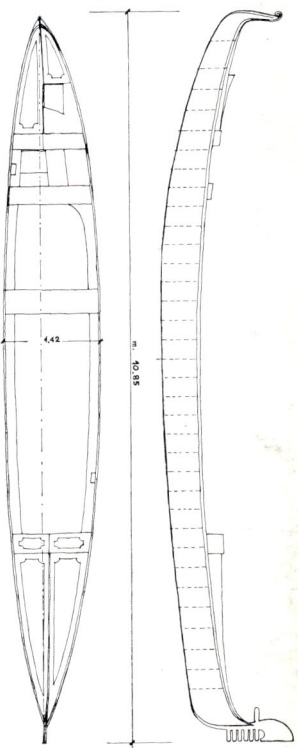

101

THE GONDOLA. The gondola is an important part of the Venetian scene, more than folklore it is a typical lagoon boat; it is the product of an ancient constructional art improved on through the centuries to create an object which is perfect both from the functional and the aesthetic point of view. It might almost be a product of industrial design or, rather, of nature, like the sea-shell. From the functional point of view the gondola embodies the characteristics of other typical lagoon boats, also very beautiful, such as the "caorlina" or the "sandalo": lightness, shallow draught, minimum resistance to water, great manoeuvrability, remarkable carrying capacity in relation to its weight and size. These characteristics are strictly bound to the topographical needs of the city. A gondola is a very tough and complex structure,

the hull alone is made of 280 pieces of seven different kinds of wood. Intended normally to be rowed by a single oar, the gondola has an asymmetrical plan, being more curved to the left than to the right, to balance the side thrust of the oar; it is also asymmetrical in section, leaning to the right, to balance the weight of the gondoliere. From an aesthetical point of view the gondola has been traditionally famous for its elegant shape; it has numerous interesting details, besides the "ferro" on the prow, there is the "forcola", rowlock of walnut wood, carved like a piece of sculpture. The poop daringly high above the water level, jutting out to take the weight of the gondoliere, with its absolutely pure line, it is perhaps from an architectural point of view the most beautiful part of the gondola.

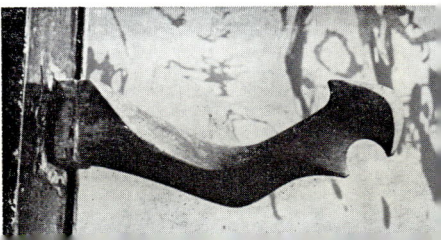

Index

Figures refer to item numbers